S0-AGC-031

# the indian parenting book

## Imparting Your Cultural Heritage

### to the Next Generation

# the indian parenting book

## Imparting Your Cultural Heritage
### to the Next Generation

## meenal pandya

3 1489 00530 6095

**MeeRa Publications**

Copyright© 2005 by Meenal Pandya

All rights reserved. No part of this book may be reproduced or transmitted in any form or by any means, electronics or mechanical system, without written permission from the author, except for the inclusion of brief quotations in a review.

Library of Congress Control Number: 2005924938
ISBN-13: 978-0-9635539-6-6
ISBN-10: 0-9635539-6-8

MeeRa Publications books may be purchased for business or promotional use or for special sales. For information, please write to:
Special Markets,
MeeRa Publications,
P.O. Box 812129
Wellesley, MA 02482.

Published by:
MeeRa Publications
P.O. Box 812129
Wellesley, MA 02482
www.MeeraPublications.com

**Note:**

To make the text reader-friendly, "he" and "she" are used alternately through-out this book, with the understanding that, in most instances, the statements will apply to both genders.

Printed in China

With love,

To:  Pujya Mummy, Pappa, and Pujya Bhai, Didi
     For teaching me everything I know about parenting!

To:  Shirali and Amoli,
     For making me experience the "value" of parenting!

# Contents

Dear Child
The day you were born
I was born too---
You as a new baby
And I, as a new mother.
From the moment you entered my world
The whole world changed forever for me.
As you opened your tiny eyes
And looked around
I too, looked around, as if,
For the first time, through your eyes---
And saw things I had never seen before.
As you learned to see
I learned to observe
As you learned to talk
I learned to listen
As you learned to walk
I learned to let go.
For both of us, the journey has just begun.
May we both keep learning together
The true meaning of love, innocence, and curiosity
But best of all, the true meaning of life.

meenal pandya

# A special note:

Although any parent or teacher who is interested in imparting Indian culture to young children can benefit from reading this book, the majority of the ideas offered in this book relate to imparting culture to children between ages four to fourteen. It is my belief that these are the most formative years in a young person's life and the kind of cultural imprint you can offer during these years will serve as a foundation for everything that they learn later in their lives.

Here is a list of readers who can benefit from this book:

- Indian families raising children outside of India
- Indian grandparents
- Families where one spouse is of Indian ancestry
- Parents of adopted children from India
- Teachers who have any student of Indian ancestry

I would also like to point out that even though there are many diverse ethnic groups and religions within India, which have influenced the cultural fiber of the society, in this book I have focused on the values that stemmed from the Hindu "way of life" because of my personal background and understanding. Also, Hinduism is practiced by over 80% of the population in India, and I believe offers the "cultural foundation"for the society.

THE INDIAN PARENTING BOOK

# Acknowledgment

A book like this is really a culmination of one's life: everything that I have learned throughout my life has somehow affected the kind of parent I have become and the kind of things I have passed on to my children. These lessons have also impacted the way I relate to them. So it is really very difficult to thank everyone who has contributed to this book. However, I would like to thank many people who made special contributions to this writing. Without you, and your contribution, this book would not have been possible.

I would like to offer special thanks to Abhay and Jaya Asthana who invited me to talk to many parents in the Balvihar programs that they organize and offered so many suggestions. I would also like to thank Dr. Mahesh Mehta whose invaluable suggestions and sharp insight on many of these issues has enriched this book in many ways. I would also like to thank many of our friends who invited me to their homes and into their lives and shared their concerns. They are Nishtha Limbachya, Hemanti and Kanchan Banerjee, Carolyn Passey, Ramesh and Manjula Patel, Rajesh and Mamta Patel, Harish and Hemadri Patel, Sanjay Mehta, Hasit and Dr. Taru Parikh, Ravi Sreedhar and Shaila Vasudev. My friend Betsy Zahniser has been a great source of support and her suggestions have enriched this book tremendously. I would like to thank Jothi Raghavan for providing me with her insight especially about Bharatnatyam dances and Ami Potter and Jayshree Vyas for their many invaluable suggestions. Ami, your help in this project was invaluable and your specific suggestions brought unique perspective to many of the issues discussed here.

Big thanks go to my daughters, Shirali and Amoli, who read several versions of this manuscript, gave their suggestions and challenged me on many levels. I also want to thank my two sets of parents who have continued to shape my life with their invisible hands even when I moved ten thousand miles away from them.

Last but not least, I want to thank my husband Atul who gave me courage and enthusiasm every time I felt the pressure of this insurmountable project. Atul, you have always stood next to me in every issue of parenting, lending your wisdom and support while respecting my feelings. And without your encouragement and support, I would not have been able to write this book.

# Introduction

A freshly-minted young psychologist started offering a
seminar for young parents. The title of his seminar was "Ten
commandments for young parents." A few years later he got
married and became a father of one child. He changed the
title of his seminar to "Ten suggestions for young parents."
After the arrival of the second child his seminar title changed
to "Ten suggested themes for young parents," and after
the arrival of his third child he stopped giving seminars.

Dear Reader,

Congratulations! The fact that you have picked up this book
shows that you are concerned about imparting your cultural heritage to your children. You want to raise culturally-balanced children: children, who not just the two of you but the entire world
can one day be proud of, children who may lead tomorrow's
world with integrity and wisdom, children who are not afraid to
stand up for the things that they believe in, children who grow
up to become the torch bearers of their cultural heritage, children who are compassionate and caring, children who embody
what is best in Indian culture and who will move forward in the
global village. These are, of course, lofty goals, but they are not
impossible. One of the blessings of being a parent is that God

has trusted you to shape a human being. Parenting is hard, but one of the most fulfilling jobs we will do in our entire life.

I wish someone had written this book twenty years ago when my husband and I were trying to raise our two daughters. Teaching them about their cultural heritage was one of the important cornerstones of how we wanted to raise them, but we did not know exactly how to go about achieving that effectively and practically. There were so many questions: questions that could not be answered by our non-Indian friends since they could not quite identify with the concerns that stemmed from our background and heritage; questions that could not be answered by friends and parents in India who were not familiar with raising children in Western culture. We felt isolated.

One day, as I walked out of the day care center —brightly decorated with Halloween pumpkins and pictures— where my eight-month-old daughter was spending her days, I wondered how on earth she will ever know about *Diwali* and I can go about teaching her. I had no problem with her celebrating Halloween, but I wanted to make sure that she also knew that around the same time there is another festival — *Diwali* — that her parents, grandparents, and cousins in India celebrate.

As young parents, we struggled at every juncture, stumbled on many issues, made several mistakes. In the process, we also realized that some of the things that we fretted so much over were not that important, while there were other issues we now wish we had paid more attention to. In short, we learned a lot in the process. I have tried to write about what we have learned, either from our own experience or learning from others around us. I have also asked hundreds of parents and their children about what they think is helping and what is not needed. So this book is enriched by the first-hand experiences of many parents.

Of course times have changed for the Indian community. Today, the community has grown by many folds and many things have become available and today's parents are beneficiary of that more-established network of extended family members, temples, and other community organizations. Yet the issues discussed in this book are eternal and useful to parents nonetheless.

Writing this book has been an act of faith for me. For a long time I struggled between two opposing forces: "Who am I to write this book?" to " Having raised two children of my own and talking to hundreds of other parents, I have learned a thing or two so it is my solemn duty to share that knowledge with today's young parents who may be facing similar problems." Finally, the second argument prevailed as several of my friends also urged me to write this book. It is neither an ultimate guide nor an all-knowing reference book. This book is about sharing ideas that either helped me, or that I wish I had known about when I was raising my children.

Of course, every parent knows that that there are no "turn-key" solutions when it comes to raising a child. Every child is different and every household is different. In fact, it is almost every parent's experience that children raised in the same household by the same parents in about the same timeframe will turn out to be quite different and will require varied ways to handle their needs and curiosity. So these ideas by no means represent a hard and fast solution. Rather, they are meant to help today's young parents to see child rearing in perspective, to sort out and analyze the many day-to-day issues that arise so that they can come to their own conclusions about what is best for their family.

Because Indian culture is very complex and dynamic, one of the important goals of this book is to help you decipher some of the misconceptions about what is considered Indian culture and to provide you with practical tools to impart what is truly valuable to our next generation. I believe that every parent has the innate sense of what is right for their children, what they want to teach them, what is right and what is wrong. Often it is either missed in the hurried life we live, or it is difficult to translate into words and actions. So this book is not to tell you what is right but to help you think your way through these issues and use some of the tips given in many chapters.

No one has to tell you that parenting is a difficult job especially when you are juggling two cultures and two careers. There are so many issues to deal with and so little time! Parenting is hard, but cultural parenting is even harder. My hope is that even if this book helps you a little in that struggle, the book has served its purpose. May God help us all in creating a better tomorrow, because parenting is all about the future – ours, theirs and every-ones.

Good luck and happy parenting

meenal pandya                    February 3, 2005

# ✿ 1 ✿
# *Cultural Parenting*

❖

To My Child

Often you will hear the word culture

And wonder what it really means:

Is it music? Is it dance?

Is it drama? Is it literature?

Is it art? Is it all of the above?

Maybe, maybe not

For

It is not the music but the feelings that you sing thru music

It is not the dance but the emotion you express thru dance

It is not the drama but the message conveyed in the drama

It is not the literature but what makes it a literature

It is not the art but what comes through that art

Your culture is your guiding light

That shows you the way

To lead your life

May your culture shine through everything you do and

Everything you achieve in life.

meenal pandya

# What is culture?

At its core, culture is what separates humans from other species. You may call culture the line drawn between animals and humans. Although human beings are essentially born with animal instincts, the difference is that we have the free will to act and think. We are given the potential to become divine. Culture, at its best, is the path that makes this journey possible. Both animals and human beings respond to instincts. For example, when hunger strikes, both will look for ways to satisfy the pangs of hunger. But culture is what tells a human being what to eat, when to eat, and how to eat. Culture also allows human beings to fine tune basic instincts. The Sanskrit word for culture is *Sanskruti* and it is referred to as the upward journey from *prakriti* (instinct or nature). Interestingly, the journey in the opposite direction from *prakriti* will take you to *vikruti* (perversion). Think of it this way: to eat when you are hungry is *prakriti* (nature), to eat when you are not even hungry is *vikruti* (perversion) and to share your food with others who may also be hungry is *sanskruti* (culture). A culture, therefore, is really refining our animal instincts and making us more human.

Different cultures of the world are really different ways to refine this journey. Every culture is born out of its civilizations' worldview and is historically based on its religion, which plays a vital role in the evolution of different cultures. It defines what is considered important in that civilization, what is at the center of its worldview, and what is the ultimate goal it is trying to achieve. That is why a culture survives and thrives on the strength of its environment, since a larger community with similar goals and a common worldview is essential in sustaining the values of the culture. There are many distinguishing characteristics of different cultures. One important distinguishing aspect of any culture is how it treats people who are either weaker or different.

Indian culture has evolved around the Hindu view of life that is based on the three pillars. They are:

▷ "Vasudhaiva Kutumbakam" (All creation is one family),

▷ every life is potentially divine, and

▷ there are many different paths to arrive at the same truth.

These three fundamental beliefs shape almost every value and behavior that we associate today as Indian culture.

## What is cultural parenting?

Cultural parenting is, in essence, helping your next generation on the path of this journey. On a more practical level, it is *what* you teach your children, *how* you teach your children and what you emphasize in your *own* life. Every act of a parent becomes a learning process and creates a cultural imprint for the child. In a homogenous society where the majority of people share similar values, cultural parenting is not a large issue simply because a child growing up in such cultures receives the same message from everyone: his parents, his teachers, his neighbors, his friends and so on. But in a multicultural society, where the values taught at home may or may not be consistent — and often may be at odds with what they hear from the outside world — a child gets different messages from different sources and is either likely to get confused, or lean toward the culture that is more dominant or convenient.

Indian parents living in the U.S. today struggle with these issues, because they intuitively know that although their heritage is very rich, and their children could benefit from that richness, they also realize the strength of the western culture and they want to make sure that their children benefit from these two very distinct influences. They know that by sheer osmosis, their children will absorb the outside culture but they fear that their children may grow up without understanding the rich heritage of their own ancestry and thereby will miss out on its value. They also fear western culture; although it has many great values such as hard work and a strong civic sense, there are other values that are diametrically opposite to what Indians value. Also, western culture can be very glamorous and may pose an overwhelming influence on children if parents do not handle young minds with tact and understanding.

Interestingly, young parents within the Indian community in the U.S. today are not a homogenous group but rather quite diverse. On one hand, some young Indian parents are themselves the children of first generation Indian immigrants. Such parents, who have learned about Indian culture secondhand, may feel the need for cultural parenting to pass on to their offspring. This is challenging, though, without knowing the depths and complexity of our culture. On the other hand, since Indian immigration to the U.S. is rather recent and ongoing, many of today's parents are new immigrants who have been raised in India. Although they absorbed these cultural values from their surroundings, they may feel ill equipped to teach it to their own children here. Then there are families where only one of the parents is of Indian descent, while the other is of a different culture. In this book, I have tried to address the needs of all of such parents.

Indians began arriving in U.S. in the late sixties and early seventies in small numbers, and the little trickle of immigration turned into a huge flow in the eighties, nineties, and beyond. Today, Indians are one of the fastest growing groups of immigrants in America, doubling in numbers every five years. Statistically, Indians are one of the most successful communities in America and are putting down deep roots in this soil. However, they need the tools to create a next generation that is culturally rich and balanced.

We need to improvise, not only because India is changing, but also because the world is getting smaller. Rules and methods that worked for our parents and grandparents may not necessarily work for us here and now. Yet, we still need to look for ways to nourish our cultural roots so that future generations can harvest the benefits that are their birthright.

Zeroing in on what we want to teach under the banner of "culture" is a very individual and often difficult choice. The world is becoming progressively global and our children are truly the first generation of citizens of this "global village." To be a global citizen, they will need to understand and balance opposing value systems. They will need to understand the "value" of each value that they will inherit from us, so they can be effective citizens of this new global community and yet have strong roots to nourish their souls and minds.

This task is made more difficult because India is also changing and unless we pick values that can cross the boundaries of time and space–in other words, values that are eternal–we might wind up teaching our children an outdated lifestyle rather than the true values of Indian culture.

So, as we can see, cultural parenting is much more than letting your children know about your cultural heritage. It is about balancing two (or may be even more) cultures, it is about being innovative and traditional at the same time, it is about being curious and yet grounded with some understanding of why you do what you do. Cultural parenting is about building bridges for future generations so that they can effectively cross the boundaries of two cultures and become happy and healthy members of both.

It should be pointed out that cultural parenting is not about superiority of one culture above another, but about understanding cultural roots so that our children can respect other cultures as well. It is said that any person who cannot respect himself cannot respect anyone else. Similarly, a child cannot appreciate other cultures unless he or she understands and respects her own. For example, a child who has understood respectful behavior in the western world will also be curious to learn what is "proper" etiquette to show respect to the elderly members of the family when she visits India. It is that sense of respect that matters more than the manner in which it can be displayed in two different cultures.

In this book, I have tried to "bring out" the issues that as parents we deal with every day and to see how we can "inject" cultural dimensions. I know that each one of us is smart enough to make the right choices for our children. Often what we need is just a nudge to steer our thinking. So in this book, you will find suggestions and analysis — but not step-by-step instructions — to choose your own path of parenting.


# Samskara: The Cultural imprint

Since we are going to talk about cultural parenting, it is essential that we understand what we mean by Samskara, the cultural currency we use to create our future generations. The word Samskara can have two meanings although both the meanings are intertwined. Rites of passage, and the ceremonies that accompany them, are often referred to as Samskara. There are sixteen important Samskaras in a Hindu life, celebrating every important passage in one's life. Samskara also means one's cultural imprint – something that happens every day in every activity where a child learns what is right and what is wrong, cultural etiquette, his or her role in the family, community and society and dharma – a code of conduct.

In this book we use the word Samskara with the latter meaning although there is a chapter devoted to rites of passage as well. It is fair to ask why bother giving Samskara to our children? Should not education, intelligence, money, and independence that we offer as parents be enough for a happy life? Of course all of those things are very important for a happy and successful life, but cultural roots can provide the nourishment and connection to an individual that education, money, intelligence and everything else may not. In fact, Samskaras provide the grace and thinking for acquiring all of the above. Samskara are like anchors that connect the individual to the family, community, society, and then to God. In the Sanskrit language the word for an individual is "vyakti" which literally means expression or manifestation. It implies that an individual is an expression of the otherwise inexpressible or "avyakta", meaning God. In other words, Samskaras give the connection to a "vyakti" (individual) to what is "avyakta" (unseen). Proper Samskaras will anchor an individual throughout his or her life, helping him or her to make choices, to make friends, to connect with the rest of the world, to know his or her own self, and to ultimately progress on the path of spirituality.

19

When we use the word Samskara in this book we are referring to the imprints on young minds that create tracks for future actions. So giving cultural roots to our children so that they remain anchored in their lives while they face inevitable ups and downs, while they make decisions large and small throughout their adult lives, while they continue their spiritual journey and while they connect to the rest of the world, is the goal of cultural parenting as well as the goal of this book.

2 

# The Value of Giving Cultural Roots

I remember meeting a young college student a few years ago who was studying at Harvard University in Boston. During his growing years, like many parents of their generation, his parents had decided that teaching him anything Indian would confuse him if his life was going to be lived in America, so they did not teach anything about India and its culture. But when he came to Harvard and his classmates started asking him questions about India, he became quite frustrated and took it upon himself to find out about his culture. His exact comment to me was, "I wish my parents had not deprived me of this rich heritage."

When you are raising your children outside of India in the 21$^{st}$ century, do you wonder why you should even bother about teaching Indian values? Aren't they going to be global citizens who will be jetting themselves from culture to culture without getting attached to any place or time? Also, isn't India – and the rest of the world – becoming more western and more homogenized than ever before? In such an environment, why bother with Indian culture at all? After all, what are cultural roots?

Today, many parents seem to be asking these questions *while* raising their kids. And rightly so. On the surface, it may make more practical sense to raise children without any cultural anchoring.

But when you scratch the surface and look deeper, you realize the value of giving your children strong, healthy cultural roots. When they become adults, their cultural roots will continue to provide nourishment, direction, a sense of belonging and a sense of self.

In the world, where boundaries are diminishing and the distances are getting smaller, and the cultures are getting more homogenized your children will need cultural roots before they find their wings. They will need more nourishing from these roots when they deal with a world full of strangers and are searching for their own identity.

Priya Agarwal, in her book, *Passage From India: Post 1965 Indian Immigrants and Their Children*, points out that "In College, a majority of second generation Indians come to terms with their Indian background and start to view it more positively." Think of it this way: the more the outside world is non-homogenous, the more one will need to draw strength from inside. And cultural roots just provide a sense of identity that keeps the nourishing possible.

There is another reason too. In this century, India is already emerging to be a very prominent world power and having your children understand and feel comfortable about their Indian roots will help them become more confident and productive members of tomorrow's world.

Indian culture is one of the richest cultures where every aspect of a human life is fully understood and every kind of growth from physical to material and spiritual is interwoven in day-to-day living. The benefits of this can be immense and immediate.

Here are some of the reasons you may want to consider when considering the value of imparting your cultural heritage to your

children. You may have your own reasons that you can add to
this list as well:

▷ Gives them a strong sense of identity and a sense of belonging

▷ Allows them to understand their background and their heritage

▷ It is their birthright

▷ It is one of the richest and most ancient cultures that has
viewed life from every angle

▷ Every sixth person in the world is an Indian so knowing
about their culture would help them create a strong identity.

▷ It will provide them the tools and the understanding to handle the ups and downs of life.

Let us help our children lead a productive, happy and healthy
life by introducing them to their cultural heritage.

# A brief history of Indian immigration in America

About thirty years ago, when a friend of mine was trying to organize her own wedding in America, she was having a difficult
time in many ways–from locating a priest who could perform
a Hindu ceremony to finding the right flowers for a garland.
The guest list consisted of the bride, the groom, the priest and
about six friends in someone's living room. This year, her son

got married with a grand ceremony in a large wedding hall in Chicago. The wedding included over five hundred people with all the intricate details including a group of traditional wedding song singers that they were able to find locally.

That is how much the Indian community in America has changed in the last three decades.

Today there are over 2.5 million Indians in America and they are one of the most successful immigrants in the history of America. According to a recent article in *National Review* magazine (Fall, 2004), their median income is $60,000 (as against the general American one, about $39,000). They boast approximately 200,000 millionaires. They are extraordinarily educated, and they are leaders in many professions. They include about 40,000 doctors—a staggering figure—to which you can add about 12,000 medical students and interns. Famous small-business owners, Indian Americans preside over nearly 40 percent of hotels in the United States. In short, this is a group of American super-achievers.

Indians are also one of the fastest growing minorities in America. They are the third largest Asian population in America. In the very short time that they have started arriving on American soil, they have achieved notable success in almost every field, ranging from academics and high technology to the motel and diamond industry. According to a recent Wall Street Journal article, Indians are the wealthiest minority in America. They have become the "model minority".

It is interesting to note how these immigrants have become a vibrant and functioning community from almost nothing in a relatively short period of time. In the mid-sixties, the first few Indians arrived in the U.S. and they really paved the way for many more to come. Many factors came into play in this community's growth. The strong family bond that most Indians have in India meant they invited family members over to enjoy the lifestyle that they had come to like and enjoy. Here is a brief overlook at how the community has changed over a period of four decades– from the 1960s to the start of the new millennium.

Although there are records of a small group of Indian farmers – mostly from the state of Punjab – having immigrated to America, in general, the Immigration Act of 1917 especially barred immigration of Asian Indians. But in 1965, when John F. Kennedy set a quota of 20,000 immigrants from each country, the real migration of Indians, as we know it today, occurred in America. So Indians are relatively new to this land of opportunity.

**Late 1960s and early 1970s**

In 1965, when America opened its gates to Indians, the first to trickle in were Indian students coming to receive higher education. The majority of these immigrants were single, educated, and they came with the goal returning to their motherland with some education, money, experience and the qualifications that would guarantee them a better livelihood in India. By the mid-seventies there were about 175,000 Indians in America.

Although these Indians were able to meet their goals of acquiring higher education and work experience, most of them did not go back for several reasons. The economic climate in India was not suitable for their aspirations; the lure of the strong American dollar was greater than they had once thought, and in the end, they realized that they themselves had changed, and readjusting to India's work and social climate would not be easy. Whatever the reasons, instead of returning permanently to India as per their original plan, they went back home for a visit, got married and brought their spouses to America to start family life in the U.S.

During this time, most places in America did not have Indian stores, temples, organizations or any such services. It meant that for every small thing, they had to resort to their homeland. This was also the time when contacting India was not that easy; it was mostly done via mail. Phone calls were expensive and difficult. Emails and other technological breakthroughs were not yet on the horizon. Teaching Indian culture or language to their children was very difficult.

**The 1980s**

The trickle of immigrants turned into a large stream in the late seventies and eighties and just kept increasing. These new immigrants – especially the ones who came in the eighties – had different reasons to migrate. They came not just for higher education but they came as family members, and they came to have a better life for themselves and their families. Also, as the numbers grew, many things changed. What started out as an all-professional group now slowly changed to include businessmen and women, writers and artists, taxi drivers and store owners. They also helped provide the community that was now growing with many essential services–from restaurants and grocery stores to priests and temples. They also started to settle down and have their own children, and sow roots. The infrastructure grew considerably.

During this time more and more stores started opening to serve the growing Indian community. As the infrastructure and the family structure grew, the roots became stronger and cultural outlets, organizations, and temples started to sprout on American soil. Today, in large cities, you can find almost anything one may need from India.

**The 1990s**

The nineties brought yet a different kind of immigrant from India. Two very powerful things happened in the early nineties. First, India opened its markets to the world, which changed both India and its economic climate. The youth of India, unlike their earlier counterparts, began to see a lot of opportunities. But most importantly, the technological revolution brought young, freshly minted graduates to the United States. In the nineties about 50% of the H-1 visa distribution was to Asian Indians. These immigrants had a more global worldview, a stronger sense of identity and a different set of needs.

During this time a lot of success stories started pouring into the media about Indian immigrants, especially in the field of computers and telecommunications. This helped the community feel stronger about their own culture and identity. The success of earlier immigrants who excelled in the fields of business, real estate, and finance also created a sense of pride within the community.

Children growing up during this time could have a better understanding about India and its culture, and had stronger ties with their family members in India due to easy access to email and telephone. The roots of the Indian community in America grew stronger and more confident.

**Now and in the future:**

Today, the mix of Indian immigrants in America is quite varied. The success of the previous generations has fueled a lot of enthusiasm into the young, which has created a more confident community. The community is growing, changing, and putting down its roots on American soil, which makes it interesting as well as challenging in trying to sort out what we consider "culturally" significant and how we give that to our next generation.

# Today's Indians as pioneers of the future society

So as the society takes root, it finds itself reinventing cultural and social norms. We, the new immigrants, are like the branches of the roots that are diving deep into the ground to find nourishment. Each one of us will travel separately in different directions searching for the cultural nourishment for this new tree that has been planted in the soil of America.

As our society grows, not only in numbers but also becomes more varied as people with different skills enter the shores of America raising children becomes slightly easier, especially in certain pockets of America such as New Jersey, California, and Chicago. The trend will continue in the future as the Indian community becomes more established with real roots. It is good to remember though, that what we pick now will stick as Indian culture for many generations to come. While we go through the process of defining what we consider important and worth preserving in Indian culture, and what we consider impractical in this land of opportunity, we are putting down roots for future generations.

# India's dynamic society

While visiting India without her parents, a teenage girl who was born and brought up in America, chose to wear an Indian outfit to a gathering assuming that it would be inappropriate to wear western clothes. To her surprise, she found herself out of place when she saw that every other girl her age was clad in a T-shirt and jeans.

One of the common complaints from Indian children who are raised in America is that they are often surprised to see that they come across more "Indian" then their cousins or peers in India when they visit India. The society in India, just as any living, breathing society is a dynamic society that is constantly changing. The India they find can be very different from the India they left behind. As the saying goes, "You can never step in the same river twice." This adds to the complexity of Indian parents, as they have to sift through changing values and find what is more permanent about India's culture so that kids growing up today can assimilate with their peers outside of India as well as in India. In some ways, the change in India is bringing its culture closer to the western ways of doing things.

It is hard to capture a living culture and impart its values to your children because a sign of any healthy culture is that it is ever-changing and dynamic. A culture that takes the demands and trends of modern society, and weaves within it what is valuable to the culture, flourishes with time.

Indian culture, being one of the most vibrant and dynamic, is ever-changing, adopting new ideas and blending them with what is most valuable. The beauty of it is that on one hand it is based on eternal values, and on the other, it has the flexibility to embrace new aspects of changing times.

I saw one very good example of this while I was visiting India during Diwali. Traditionally, in the Gujarati merchant community, accounting books are honored and worshipped during Diwali. This time I noticed that the merchants were including the computer along with the books, in their pooja. To me, this showed that the community was able to accept and integrate the new technology and were willing to see it as an extension of all that is sacred in business.

This is similar to performing the pooja of one's car on Dusera (Vijaya dasmi), a day when traditionally, kings honored their horse as a symbol of transportation. Even with changing times, and modern means of transportation, people still continued to celebrate the spirit of worshipping their mode of transportation.

It is hard to capture such a dynamic culture unless we look at the very core of why we do what we do and see how the same goal can be accomplished when the time, place, or any other parameters change. As immigrant parents, it is vital that we understand this clearly so that we do not become "frozen" into the image of our culture and disregard the ever-changing nature of it.

3 🪷

# *Values: Deciding What, Why, and How*

Once we become parents everything changes: our worldview, our sense of what is right, and even how we view the news. In fact, it is quite surprising to see how we change as soon as we become parents. I have seen so many young couples completely oblivious to their cultural background suddenly searching for their roots, their beliefs, their ancestors, and their value system as soon as they become parents. This is especially true of immigrant parents, for whom, the task of raising children in an environment where their own culture is not living and breathing is daunting.

In fact, in many families, this is the cause of major stress since both partners may have a different idea of what might be considered Indian values. Further, many of the values that we may consider Indian are in reality universal values. For example, truth and honesty are taught, respected, and desired in every culture and though we may have learned them from our Indian parents, and therefore consider them Indian values, they are shared by all cultures.

Often what we consider an Indian value may be just a way to behave. For example, giving respect to elders is not uniquely Indian, but *how* you show respect may be different in each culture. So even though the values may be similar, each culture may have different ways of expressing them.

Then, there are unique Indian values that we want our children to inherit as we feel that these values will not only help them connect to their cultural roots, but also help them to lead a happy, healthy and more fulfilled life.

As parents, perhaps our first job is to identify true Indian values, and then to figure out a way to teach them. In the words of one wise grandmother, "Visualize what you want to see in your child twenty-five years from now, and start acting that way today." Your values have to translate into actions, and your actions must reflect what you believe in.

Let us first examine which are universal values and which are truly Indian values.

## Universal or human values

Almost every parent in the world, whatever their cultural or economic background, wants to teach good values to their offspring. In some ways, these values are easy to emphasize because no matter where you live in the world, everyone shares them with you. Due to the universal nature of these values, parents find that the neighborhood, the schools, and the community all form a support system to reinforce the same values. For example, honesty is one such value; no matter where you live, the message to become an honest human being will be given by everyone. Of course, the bottom line is that a child will learn what is practiced in his or her own household. The easy part in teaching these values comes from the fact that when your child steps outside of your home, these values are not being ridiculed nor questioned. He or she will get the same message from everyone around him or her. Reinforcement is the key to teaching any value.

Here are some of the most common universal values:

▷ Truth

▷ Honesty

▷ Compassion or Love

▷ Fairness and Justice

▷ Respect

▷ Love

▷ Courage

▷ Self-Reliance

▷ Chastity

▷ Discipline

▷ Kindness

These universal values are respected, desired, expected, and reinforced by almost every culture and therefore are easier to learn. (A note: if you are interested in finding out how to teach these values to your children, you may want to read *Teaching your children Values* by Linda and Richard Eyre. There is another book *Raising Good Children from Birth through Teenage Years* by Thomas Lickona).

# Indian values

Uniquely Indian values are principles based on the Hindu view of the world. The basis of most Indian values is the idea of "Vasudhaiva Kutumbakam" meaning the entire world is one family.

The idea that God resides in every being, seen and unseen, is also a strongly Indian concept. These two pillars give birth to the notion of tolerance, compassion, interdependence, and reverence for life on earth.

To imprint these values, Hinduism prescribes ten sets of Yama (Restraints), and ten sets of Niyama (Code of Conduct) that one should observe in order to lead a happy and productive life. These Yama and Niyama pretty much create the core value system for Hindus. The ten Yama are: nonviolence, truthfulness, non-stealing, celibacy until marriage, forgiveness, steadfastness, compassion, honesty, moderate consumption and purity of mind, body and speech. The ten Niyamas are: remorse, contentment, giving, faith, worship, understanding scriptures, cognition, upholding sacred vows, recitation of scriptures and discipline.

These Yama and Niyama give birth to many of the values that form the essence of Indian culture.

Some of these values are discussed here in detail.

**Sacredness (Reverence)** Hindus believe that the divine spark resides not only in every human being, but also in every thing in nature, including animals and birds, rivers and mountains. Sacredness is all-pervading. Reverence towards different everyday objects also influences our life in a very unique way. For example, if your feet accidentally touch a book, you ask for forgiveness from the book, since books are givers of *"vidya"* or knowledge. How do you teach your child that their textbooks are sacred since they offer knowledge and therefore are representative of the *Goddess Saraswati*? Instilling the notion of sacredness and showing respect even towards inanimate objects like books can be taught in many ways. Here are some suggestions:

▷ At the beginning of their school year, place their textbooks at the family shrine and offer some prayers together.

▷ On certain festivals such as Navratri, ask them to bring their books to the prayer room for prayers.

▷ Talk about their teachers with respect.

▷ Establish some rules about dinnertime or prayer time or prayer room.

▷ Show that you respect everything—not only the environment, but also the property of others.

**Interdependence and not independence**

The idea that you are part of the entire universe–what happens around you affects you, and what you do, affects the environment is a Hindu view of life. The interconnectedness between an individual and the entire cosmos is very systematically integrated in a Hindu life. Of course, most people who practice this are unaware of the subtle connectedness. But it is reflected in every facet of life even today. So how do you teach this interconnectedness to your children? It may be by raising the child's awareness of how his or her actions impact others.

▷ While reading a book to your child, ask him or her how the character may be feeling.

▷ Point out how many people are involved in a simple task such as having breakfast. Someone has to go to get the ingredients, someone has to prepare, someone is putting it in the store shelf, etc.

▷ Teaching children the importance of helping others.

## The Concept of Family

> I asked an American woman of Irish descent married to an
> Indian almost for over three decades, what she considered was
> the most significant value of Indian culture. Her answer was
> emphatic and clear. She said that she thinks the Indian family
> system is so strong and special that unless one experiences
> it first-hand, it is hard to fathom the depth and width of it.

The concept of family is integral and fundamental to Indian culture. There is ample evidence of concept that the entire world is one family.

Extended families are the norm in most of India. The family encompasses a much larger unit which is closely knit, and in it, each family member plays a clear role. An outsider is often quickly absorbed in the family as the "son" or "daughter" or "uncle" or "aunt." In fact, every relationship has a unique word for it, so as soon as you call someone "mausi" she becomes your mother's sister and is offered a "place" in the hierarchy of the family system. Of course in modern India, many of these roles are questioned, and a "new" sense of nuclear family is replacing some of the ancient ideas. However, making young children more aware of their larger family can be done in several ways.

▷ Celebrate the birthdays of grandparents, cousins and other relatives who do not live with you.

▷ Look at the family tree, if you have one, and show where your child fits into that larger family.

▷ Instead of simply calling a relative "uncle" or "aunt", make it a point to use the precise Indian name for the relationship.

## The Concept of the Individual

Similarly, the concept of an individual is also very different in Indian culture. From a philosophical point of view, the concept of an individual and the relationship with the community takes the form of a spiral shape. The individual is at the center, but he extends himself out to connect to the family, the community, and to society at large. There is little emphasis on the self; instead, the role of interdependence is stressed, while independence is given a back seat. This concept is at odds with the western world where there is much more emphasis on the self and self-growth, resulting in strong independent individuals who may not necessarily know how to operate in an interdependent environment.

## Duty vs. Rights

Duties and rights are really two sides of the same coin; you cannot have one without the other. For every right there is a corresponding duty. And, in Indian culture, duty is defined as dharma. Western culture also understands this relationship between duty and rights clearly. The difference, often, between the two cultures is on the emphasis. Indian culture, at least in its ideals, puts the emphasis on duties whereas in the West, the emphasis is on rights. While raising a child, our problem comes when we are trying to stress duties in a culture where the media and one's peers are busy asserting rights. As parents, we struggle with how to cope with these seemingly opposite forces.

Once we understand this relationship and the emphasis, we can teach our children the value of duties and the benefits of rights and how the two really go hand in hand. This will allow our children to grow up with the awareness that every time they feel deprived of their rights, they can check to see if they have first fulfilled their own duty properly. Of course, there is nothing wrong in standing up for your rights as long as you are clear as to what duties must follow.

**The Concept of Maryada:**

Maryada is a very loaded Indian word which is hard to translate in English with precision. Maryada literally means "knowing your limits" but it is much more than that. Maryada is also a sense of respect by which your behavior is defined. It extends from your selection of clothes to how you speak and even how you fight for what is right. Maryada is a self-imposed limit that comes from within and that is something that you choose not to cross because it is not who you are.

Since the concept of Maryada stems from factors such as proper etiquette, respect, and core values, parents may find it difficult to put their hands on what is appropriate behavior. Actually, Maryada and respect are intertwined in some ways. As parents, what we are really interested in teaching our children is that sense of Maryada so that respect will come automatically. For example, if a child knows that it is okay to disagree with parents, it is also important to emphasize that the style of his disagreement is governed by his or her sense of Maryada.

**Scriptures, Yoga, Meditation, and Pranayam**

Many Indian parents are interested in teaching the philosophical cornerstones of Indian culture to their children, and fortunately, meditation and yoga have recently become quite popular in America so children may learn many basic ideas from the outside environment as well. However, Hindu scriptures such as the *Bhagavad Gita*, the *Ramayana* and the *Mahabharata* can be learned either in the home environment or from the community.

Teaching about scriptures is both easy and hard at the same time. Luckily, stories, books and videos on the subject abound, and because Hindu religion is filled with mythological stories that are based in philosophy, they are also very accessible to young children. For parents who are born and brought up in America and may not have direct contact with these classic texts, it can be a fun way to learn as well.

In the end, it is up to you to decide what you consider as a uniquely Indian value. The important thing is that you identify for yourself those values that *you* want to emphasize in your home and in your community–values your child will not receive from the outside environment, but are those you consider important enough to pass on to your next generation.

## Choosing your values

One of the most crucial aspects of child rearing is to identify the values that our children will need to inherit. Often parents do this without consciously choosing them; they just get emphasized in your everyday living. Those values that predominate your family life will take root in your children and these are values they will inherit in the end.

Here are some points to consider:

**Why is this value important to me?**

Some introspection is necessary regarding what one values and why. Unless the value that you are trying to pass on to the next generation rings true to you and has been a part of your life, it may be difficult to teach. Do your own self-sorting in order to arrive at what is important.

**Am I a good example of that value?**

Children learn mostly from observing our own behavior. If they perceive a difference between your words and your actions, you might lose credibility no matter how right you are or how convincing your argument.

**What do my values mean to me?**

Often values are couched in terms that can be either misleading or loaded. Values such as kindness or caring are so commonly used that their true meaning is lost in generalities. Having a clear idea about how you define a value will help you become consistent and effective parents.

**Can I show the value of these values?**

After all, we all want to do not only what is right but also what helps us in the long run. Any value that has a potential to bear good fruits – even in the long run – may have a higher chance of being appreciated and practiced by children. For example, if a child sees that by sharing she is not only able to enjoy her own things but also has access toys belonging to others; she may find herself more willing to share. Similarly, showing respect towards someone also means that they will be respectful to you in turn.

**Values can be conflicting**

Often there are values that are at odds with each other. It is not easy to be assertive and at the same time be considerate. When you come across such opposing values, help your child think through the options clearly and come to a decision. This is the true test of values—when to be assertive, and when to give precedence to the needs of others.

**Are these values universal?**

Values that have a universal resonance can be taught with relative ease when you find the role models, books, and movies to reinforce them. Hard work has universal appeal and can be relatively easily emphasized Take advantage of the many tools available in the mainstream media to teach universal values.

**Emphasize that nothing of value comes easy**

At the core of value building is choosing the "right" way. Remind everyone including your own self that what may be easy may not be right and by the same token, doing the right thing may not be easy. Telling a lie may be easy but often you need to be brave to tell the truth.

**Point out that values are for strong people**

Values are for strong individuals and in turn, values provide strength to individuals. Emphasize that most values require strong character. Children are attracted to the idea of being strong. Take advantage of it to teach positive values. When children understand that, they may be more inclined to take the "hard" option.

**Reinforce, when you see positive values being practiced**

Take the opportunity to appreciate or acknowledge any instance when a child has practiced the value. Often when someone speaks the truth, we take it for granted. By recognizing the courage or sacrifice involved in your child's choice to speak the truth, gives a very strong and positive message to the child, and they feel proud of their actions. For example, sharing a new toy may be difficult but if you see your child sharing, make it a point to appreciate her when she does. Such reinforcing of values even works with adults.

**Watch out for your own inconsistencies**

We were watching the movie *Gandhi* together, when my daughter made a negative comment about Gandhi's bald head. I took that opportunity to explain to her that we should not judge a person by their looks or hairstyle, but instead pay attention to their character and actions. The following weekend, as we cruised around Harvard Square, I noticed a group of youngsters with punk hairstyles, and I blurted out how awful their hairstyle looked. My daughter reminded me of my own earlier comment about how we should look beyond anyone's hairstyle and looks. That was a sharp reminder to me of the inconsistencies in my own value system. Children are very sharp and find these kinds of discrepancies in their parents' behavior immediately. If you are open and admit to your mistake, your child will respect you and the value; if not, they will question both your beliefs and your behavior.

**Be consistent in what you emphasize**

A friend of mine loved to compare her children with everyone else's. Depending upon the person she was talking to, she would change what she felt important. For example, after meeting a friend whose daughter was a great soccer player, she came home and asked her daughter why she was not as good a soccer player. But the next weekend after meeting a child with high SAT scores, she demanded academic excellence from her daughter. If what you believe is the most important fluctuates all the time, your child will get confused about what you really value. Give consistent messages about what values are important to you, and set clear standards.

**Be reasonable**

Even when we all know what is right and we mean to do the

right thing, there are times when weakness takes over. When you find your child faltering, be patient. Do not start assigning labels because negative labels have a way of sticking. For example, if you find that your child did not tell you the truth, instead of saying that he is a liar, tell him that you recognize that it must have pained him a lot to act dishonestly and in the future he may find enough courage to tell the truth.

# You two working as a team

While reading the first draft of this book a young father with two children commented that this book should be given to couples at the time of their wedding as that is the beginning point of effective parenting. I think he is right. Parenting begins before we really become parents.

While doing research for this book, I was surprised to find how many spouses have opposing views when it comes to parenting styles. Not only does each parent have different ideas about what should be taught, but how it should be taught also differs. These differences seem to get intensified when it comes to what constitutes Indian culture. I found out that one of the biggest hurdles most parents face in raising children is having disagreements about what values are important to teach to children. We are all the products of our circumstances and environment and our parenting style is mostly based on how we were raised as children. Since the husband and wife typically come from different backgrounds, not to mention being of a different gender, their childhood experiences differ greatly. Add to this the fact that often two partners may come from different economic backgrounds. All such factors affect how we view parenting.

One of the most important aspects of successful parenting is to blend two seemingly different styles and arrive at an understanding of how it should be handled. Since each parenting style may have its own benefits, by blending the two, your children may truly reflect your household –one that is built by the two of you.

▷ Be open and clear with each other

▷ Understand each other's background

▷ Respect each other's differences

▷ Communicate

▷ Make sure that your child knows that you will both speak in one voice

▷ Find areas where you both have similar ideas

▷ Be realistic

Even after you and your partner have talked about differences, these issues will pop up often in the struggles of everyday life. Here are some pointers to help you deal with them as they come up:

**Be vigilant**

Whoever said that children are innocent never had any children. Parents know that from a very early age, children find out how to get things their way. In an extended family, they know exactly who will give what and at what time! So as soon as they find out that their parents disagree on an issue, they will know how to use that disagreement to their advantage! Even if this is not true in your family, as parents you are better off talking about your differences and being respectful of each other's views.

### Decide ahead of time who will decide what

If you two have difficulty coming to a common decision, one way to address that is by deciding ahead of time who will be in charge of what areas. For example, mom may make clothing decisions while dad may have the final say on vacation choices. By deciding ahead of time, you can take advantage of your own strengths and weaknesses instead of letting children exploit your strengths and weaknesses.

**Discover yourself** Remember that raising children will test many of your beliefs. Think of this as a journey to discover yourself and be ready to be pleasantly surprised. Once you embark, you will find you are on a path of growing up. After all, you do not want to raise copycats; you want to raise individuals.

### Have open discussions, not arguments

Children learn a lot when they find out that their parents have differing views on important matters but are able to discuss them openly and maturely. Not only will it teach them to respect opposing views as an adult, but they will also learn how to respectfully disagree. The important thing is that once they know that their parents are willing to express their views as well as listen to those of others, they will learn to respect opposing views without feeling threatened by them.

### Speak in one voice

Children know when there is conflict. Make sure that the child knows that ultimately you both will speak with one voice. As one young father said very nicely, "As soon as my son asks me something, I tell him to wait until I find out what Mom has to say." And his wife does the same thing. She will always say, "Have you asked Daddy yet?"

**Respect each other's opinion**

Instead of being critical of each other's parenting style, try to see the benefit of that style. For example, if your partner is much stricter than you are, that disciplinary style will benefit your child as much as your own softer approach will. After all, if both of you are very strict, you will have a very stiff family atmosphere and if both of you are easy on discipline, children may not learn the value of working hard. The trick is to decide which issues are worth disciplining and where it is okay to relax. Having a balance of opposites by seeing the value in what two parents bring to the household makes it beneficial for everyone.

# Imparting your values

Imparting values is neither easy nor a short-term assignment. It is something that happens every day with every interaction that we have with our children – and others, in their presence. These two chapters offer general and practical tips to reach the goal that you have as parents.

**Be subtle**

Values, by their very nature, are subtle and can only be imparted subtly. They are best absorbed from the environment. As every parent knows, children do not learn from being lectured but from being immersed into an environment and observing habits from their parents. Create an environment within your home that carries the values that you cherish. From the kind of pictures you hang on your walls to the kind of discussion that hums around your dinner table, you teach children about values.

**Be open to questions**

Fortunately, Indian heritage is so powerful that the more one searches for an answer, the more impressed one can be by the sheer wisdom of our ancestors and the beauty of our culture. The trick is to make our children curious enough to ask questions – even tough questions. We have to remember that they are not trying to hurt our feelings if they sound disrespectful of our ways of doing things or our ways of praying. They are simply searching. This is, of course, more evident in their teen years.

**Be prepared**

Knowing a bit about what you want to teach them always helps. Be prepared to explain what you know and be eager to search for answers together on what you do not know. Instead of saying "That is the way it has been," say, "Let us find out why that is the way it has been." More importantly, accept what is not acceptable. Over a period of time, much deterioration has entered in Indian culture and we should be willing to accept them as such, instead of trying to defend them.

**Be clear**

Understand what you value and why. We all carry a different picture of India in our heads. We have a variety of ideas about our culture and what should be imparted to our children. Often we may be confused about what are the core values that we want our children to inherit. Is it our food habits? Is it our religious practice? Is it our style of clothing? Do we want them to duplicate our way of showing respect? The clearer we are about what is important to us, and why, the more we will be able to explain and emphasize.

**Be creative**

Imparting values that are not consistent with the outside environment requires that we, as parents, become more creative about how we go about introducing concepts and customs. For example, for a child growing up in India, celebrating Diwali may come naturally because of the environment. However, outside of India, we need to find ways to celebrate so that a child can relate to and can enjoy with his friends. This requires creativity and resourcefulness.

**Get involved**

From your child's playgroup to your neighborhood picnic, try to get involved as much as possible. The more informed and involved you are in your child's life outside of your home, the more you will be able to influence her surroundings. For example, it may be wonderful to teach your child yoga at home, but it may be even more effective if you can volunteer to teach it to the neighborhood kids.

**Enjoy**

Play together, sing together, and read together. Young children especially thrive on their parent's attention and time. Enjoy time together doing everything from playing to reading together. Skip an exercise class once a week to spend half an hour dancing in your family room with your children to the music of their choice. Plenty of opportunities lurk behind these activities to teach about the culture and values that you cherish. For example, coloring a picture of Ganesha or a map of India together, may go a long way in learning about Ganesha or the part of India in which you grew up.

**Demonstrate**

Live the value you want your children to learn. If you try to teach the value of respect but often talk in disrespectful language about others, it will be difficult for your child to learn to be respectful. This is true for almost any value you want to impart. Your behavior will speak louder than your words.

**Utilize technology**

Luckily for today's Indian parents, there are videos of mythological stories such as *Ramayana* and *Mahabharata*, Raja *Harishchandra* and *Chankya*, websites that inform about Indian culture and CD-ROMs that can teach your children about ancient history. Use technology to help you create an environment that will impart information.

**Relax and enjoy**

Often we parents take our role of teaching our heritage too seriously. Think about it. If our children enjoy our company and want to do more things with us, the longer time we will have to influence their thinking. Trust yourself and the sustaining power of your heritage. As long as you can keep your children genuinely interested in searching, they will come to the right answers on their own.

# Character building

**What is character building and how is it done?**

The dictionary defines the word character as moral integrity or a special trait of a person. Character is something that flows in your veins. So how do you build moral integrity? That is a tough call. Actually, character building is really at the core of cultural parenting since character is the core of one's being. It defines everything we do in life, how we do it, the kinds of activities we choose, the friends we make, and the enemies we create. It essentially defines us, who we are. Character is a reservoir of inner strength, and in times of need we tap into this reservoir to derive energy.

Although our character is shaped with every action we take, and every encounter we make, and every person we meet, most of who we are is imprinted during our childhood and youth. That is why the role of parents and teachers is very crucial in character building. Character building is practicing your values, day in and day out, so that they become part of you. So your values create the basis of character building, but living the values provides you with strength of character.

How strongly you believe in these values and how far you are willing to go when you are being put to the test is really the measure of your character. For a child, these values are learned values. Once they start to "own" these values they can derive strength from, and will be willing to "fight" for them. That, in essence, is character building.

Just as a building is built brick by brick, character in a person can only be built day by day, action by action and incident by incident. Character building is something that is highly stressed in Indian culture because, in the final analysis, if individuals uphold their values with strength and wisdom, the world becomes a better place. From Sri Rama to Mahatma Gandhi, the most admired quality of any human being is how he or she has upheld values and how a strong character of *tyaga* (renunciation) and *bhakti* (devotion) have been demonstrated, instead of giving in to desires and weaknesses. In every piece of literature in India, in every ideal, and in every message that goes to children, character has been emphasized. Unfortunately, at times the bar is raised so high, that a large gap is created between what is expected and what is practical and thereby a sense of hypocrisy may be created.

Nonetheless, as parents our goal is to cultivate the best character in our children, while pointing out to them that ideals are like stars, you may never reach them but you still chart your journey keeping them in mind.

Here is what we can do to help our children build character.

**Through example**

The best way for a child to learn about good character is through your own example. Children may or may not listen to what their parents have to say but they watch them intently. As it has been said many times throughout this book, your actions will speak louder than your words. Your children will imitate your behavior –like it or not – so in many ways character building is just living your own life as you want them to live theirs. Make sure that your life reflects the values you value.

**Through family stories**

One of the most effective ways of character building is to share stories from your own families if you are lucky enough to have and know such stories. Share how a grand uncle had fought a just war, or how your grandmother had risked her life telling the truth during riots in the city. Pick out such stories, if you are lucky enough to have had them told to you, and tell those stories at dinnertime, at bedtime and at family gatherings. Little children feel a sense of pride and a sense of identity when they hear how their great grandfather had achieved something and they try to imbibe those values in themselves.

**Through cultural stories**

Stories play a very central role in imparting values and building character. Read stories from *Panchtantra* and other sources to your children when they are young. Stories work wonderfully well till the age of about nine or ten – the time before they start questioning everything and the time before the outside world influences them.

**Through films and videos**

Films and videos are the modern arms of storytelling and their visual and sound effects create more lasting images. Choose films and videos that enhance what you want them to learn. For example, after age twelve or thirteen movies like *Gandhi* or *Buddha* work better. For young children, stories of the *Ramayana* and the *Mahabharata* in video form help them understand their culture and the importance of standing for one's *Dharma*. There is a lot of wonderful fiction that can have a lasting impact on growing children. for example *Anne of Green Gables* can help a young girl learn to be forthright and honest. A sense of self is developed through such powerful films.

**Through shows and drama**

Often shows and drama are based on real-life stories or drawn from them. Such shows can be very powerful to those of a young, impressionable age. You can reap the positive benefits of these entertaining activities.

**Absorption through all the senses**

Unfortunately too much cynicism creeps into our children's lives through media, the entertainment world, and even books. Although cynicism has the advantage of weeding out what is extravagant, filling our children's environment with cynicism can do a disservice to their overall growth. Surround your household with what is positive, life sustaining and uplifting. Let your children feast on these positive influences unconsciously.

**Through interactions with spiritual and social leaders**

There are plenty of opportunities for parents to create interactions with spiritual and social leaders while their kids are of an impressionable age. Use these opportunities as much as possible and let your children interact, ask questions, and observe them. These are the people who can influence your children tremendously.

**Practice**

Of course the best way to teach your child to stand up for something is to let him practice it in his or her life. Opportunities come up every day to tell the truth, to be honest, to give up something for someone else, to be fair to someone, to care for someone. Let your children rise to these occasions and see them become stronger inside.

# How to deal with a child's resentment

One of the biggest battles parents face–this comes up anytime we have a seminar or discussion–is not what to teach (parents usually know what they would like their children to learn) but how to overcome their children's resentment toward learning something that is not part of mainstream culture, or part of what the child considers "cool". This is especially true during the teenage years when, predictably, children would rather be cool and be just like everyone else than be different in any way.

Every child is different and what may work wonderfully well with one child may not work with the other. I cannot pretend to know the exact formula that would work on every child every time. There are, however, some techniques that I have learned over a period of time by talking to other parents, children, and working with my own children that I would like to share with you here.

**Start early**

If there is one magic pill that works wonders, it is this: start early. I cannot emphasize it more. Young children generally accept without question; in other words they do not have an "attitude." The earlier you start with anything that you would like your child to learn, the better it will be. As many parents know, teen years are the worst time to teach anything different if the child is not willing to learn. So, not surprisingly, in most families, tension begins when the child turns twelve or thirteen.

**Timing is everything**

No matter how crucial and beneficial your suggestion is, if it is offered at a time when your child is not receptive, your efforts will go to waste. Tune into your child's receptive moods and your input will go much farther.

**Say it and leave it**

Children are smarter than we give them credit for. They know what you are trying to say and why, more often than not. So instead of hammering on an issue, and thereby implying that he or she needs to be told often, just say it and leave it at that. Let the child feel like he was given an option and that you trust his intelligence.

**Use love or logic**

Use your judgment and your child's age to decide if you are better off using love or logic. Older children will be more willing to buy your argument if it makes logical sense to them. Younger children – usually seven or younger – are more likely to respond to coaxing and praising.

**Know why**

Knowing why you would like things done in a certain way, or why certain behavior brings better results, will work in your favor. Know why you would like your children to do things your way. Be clear in your own thinking and your confidence will be communicated to your children.

# Creating balance between two cultures

## Assimilation vs. Alienation

*As an immigrant parent, one of the key issues, while raising children is how much to assimilate with the mainstream culture (assimilation) and how much to give the unique aspects of your own culture (alienation). Every action, every small decision, when you examine it closely, boils down to making a choice: Do I want to assimilate or alienate? For example, when you decide what to give your children for lunch at school you can choose to give them sandwiches or insist that they take Indian food for lunch. By making a choice you are either making a decision to assimilate or alienate your child from his peers. Neither choice is more correct than the other; it is just a matter of knowing where you stand and why. Too much assimilation will lead to complete dilution of your culture, while too much alienation will lead to isolation for your children from the mainstream culture. As a parent, your insight and skill will help them walk this fine line – now and always. Make your choice with clear understanding about why you are choosing what you are choosing.*

One of the trickiest parts of raising an Indian child in America – or for that matter anywhere outside of India – is to create a balance between two cultures. Theoretically at least, it may be easy to raise a child who is completely immersed in Indian culture or it may be easy to completely let go of Indian cultural roots. Raising a child who values and respects *both* cultures, and has created his or her own balance, demands both skill and understanding.

So how do you bring that balance to your children's upbringing? It cannot happen if your own life lacks that balance. Search within yourself. What is it that you like and respect about America? What have you learned here? Make sure that you talk about these aspects of America while you mention nice things about India. It is respecting and understanding, enjoying and appreciating different aspects of these two cultures that will translate into the balance that you are looking for and where your children will flourish.

Seek out what you like about America. Western culture is equally rich in its literature, music, art, and science. It also is great in other things such as respecting individuals and volunteering.

Over and above the everyday choices you make that will assimilate your children into the mainstream culture, here are some of the specifics that you can watch out for in your household:

**Learn about festivals, their origin, their historical significance, and customs**

> The more you take an interest in the culture of your host country, the more effective you will be in raising balanced children. For example, Thanksgiving is really a holiday to honor immigrants. As new immigrants, we can celebrate Thanksgiving with vigor even if we do not eat meat and would not cook turkey. Take the essence of this and other holidays and see how you can make it your own.

**Take interest in the history and culture of America**

Although Indian parents who are brought up in America may be more familiar with the history and cultural fine points, it is important for recently-arrived immigrants to get familiar with some of the cultural icons.

### Read classics

Western culture is endowed with beautiful and enriching children's literature. Familiarize yourself with that if you are not familiar. One of the easiest ways to learn about this is to visit your local library and ask your librarian who will be a great resource.

### Visit cultural and historic museums

Every large or small city in America is filled with nice museums that are informative, entertaining and enjoyable. Take many trips to these museums while your children are young. Celebrate their birthdays and other special days in these museums. It will be a very enriching experience for your children as well as for you.

### Go to concerts

Musical concerts and shows bring out the beauty of western culture. Especially around Christmas and holiday times, there are plenty of nice shows and concerts that you can attend. Make it a family tradition to go to these events at least once a year.

### Watch classic movies together

The same goes for many classic movies. During wintertime, make it a family event to sit and watch these movies together.

### Listen to music

From Beethoven to Mozart, there are gifted musicians who have enriched western classical music. Take advantage of this beautiful gift to share timeless music with your children.

### Be open and curious yourself

Your children will learn from you. If they see you demonstrate an interest in learning new things, they will follow your example.

**Watch what you say about any culture**

Stay away from making sweeping remarks about any culture. You may not believe how many parents make such remarks without realizing the harm that they are doing to themselves as well as their children. In most instances it may not be true and also because your children will see you as being prejudiced and then every comment that you make will be seen as coming from that prejudice. When your children see you being balanced about what you like in each culture, they learn to respect each culture for what it has to offer. Think of it this way: the two cultures that your children inherit are like two parents that are given. By understanding what is good in each one of the parents, children learn to respect the differences, make their own judgments and yet love both parents. By belittling the other parent, you are forcing the child to take sides.

# Equality begins at home: raising boys and girls

While conducting a seminar of Indian youth, I was surprised to find most of the girls — about half of the total number of attendees — complained that their parents treat their brothers differently and have separate rules for girls and boys within the same family.

Treating men and women as equals, is a relatively new social concept in the long history of human civilization. Traditionally the roles of men and women were different and well defined to make the best use of different strengths of both the genders. Modern times have created a society where these roles have merged. Yet parenting has not kept pace with changes in the society. And that is why in today's world where a lot of lip service is paid to equality, there still remain subtle differences when it comes to practicing such values. Even the mass media and other popular outlets try to "cash in" on these differences. It is to our benefit to be vigilant about our behavior and what happens within our homes.

Historically Indian culture has put women on the higher pedestal by saying "Yatra Naryaastu Pujyante, Ramante Tatra Devta" meaning "Where women are respected, Gods reside." However, due to a tremendous deterioration since Vedic times, when women enjoyed equal status in every aspect of the life, today's status of women in India leaves a lot to be desired. India is not alone in treating men and women differently and these issues are faced by almost every society today. Many of our values and ideas are shaped by what we see around us and we are all trying to adjust to emerging new roles for men and women in our society.

As parents, we are faced with these issues such as how we raise our sons and daughters and how our values, shaped in the past, bring out actions while we are making day-to-day decisions.

Look at your own behavior closely. Sometimes, there are hidden messages that our children receive from others and from us that may tell them otherwise. These subtle messages often tell our children that there are different expectations placed on boys than on girls. Does this happen in your house? The following list is just for you to check what is happening in your own household. By the way, the points I have raised here do not necessarily imply any preferences, it just points out the hidden differences in our own attitude on this important child-rearing issue.

**When buying toys**

Even for infants and very young children, our attitude is reflected when we buy toys. What kind of toys do you buy for your daughter? Do you buy dolls and things that require more nurturing? What kinds of toys do you choose for your sons?

**While playing board games**

The kinds of games we play with our children can also be based on their gender since board games reflect the kind of expectations we have from our children. Do we want them to be strong? Smart? Funny? Informed? Do you play the same games with your sons as with your daughters?

**While reading books**

Books are a very effective way to impart values that we feel are important. Do we choose the same kind of books for our sons and daughters or do we prefer different books? Next time you buy a book for a child think about what influences your decision.

**Setting curfew time**

Most teenagers complain about the curfew time set by their parents but more importantly, the difference in curfew times that parents set for brothers and sisters. If you are worried about their well being, do you convey the sense of equal responsibility to your sons and daughters?

**Dating**

Often parents set different rules for girls and boys in the same family for dating. A parent who may be more open to the idea of a son dating may be less willing to let a daughter go on a date. How do you feel about your children dating? When the time comes, would you set the same rules?

### When going on vacation

When you go on vacation, do you expect more help from your sons than your daughters? Do you choose different activities for them depending upon their gender or do you let them try the same kinds of activities? Vacations are some of the times when different roles are more clearly identified within a family.

### Expecting help around the house

Ditto for expecting help around the house. Often girls complain that they are expected to help out more around the house then their brothers. Boys often think that they are expected to help out much more with the yard work than their sisters. Does this happen in your household?

### Teaching Indian culture

Once I was at a cultural show organized by an Indian organization. It was quite interesting as well as eye-opening to notice that girls presented most of the cultural items. While enrolling our children to learn Indian cultural activities it is easier to find things that are appropriate for girls than for boys. Do you seek out activities that can also help your sons grow culturally?

### While helping them make career choices

Of course, making a career choice is one of the most important decisions of one's life. When career choices are being discussed in your home, not just for your own children but for their older cousins and your friend's children, do you consider different options for boys and girls or do you emphasize the same standards? Your opinions matter to your children – regardless of what they say openly.

Here are some of the tips to create an equal household:

### Respect each child for who he or she is

Look for unique attributes of your child and give him or her the tools to make the best use of that.

## Be a good role model

A caring father teaches his son how to show love and care while a strong mother helps impart to their daughters a sense of self-respect. See how your own role helps shape your children's identity of who they are and what can they expect from the other gender. A son who has witnessed his father always respecting his mother is not likely to disrespect other girls in school.

# 4

# *Simple Things That Go a Long Way*

## It all begins with a name

" A rose by any other name...." We have all heard it enough times to know what is coming. But is it true? It may be true for a rose, or a violet, or a table – things that do not identify themselves with their names – but for people, especially children, whose first and foremost identification comes from their names, a name has a profound significance. No wonder parents-to-be and new parents – everywhere in the world – often spend days if not months searching for that unique and special name for their newborn baby.

As many of us know, it is not easy. Finding a name that is special to both of you, a name that is culturally and socially tied to your roots and yet is unique, a name that sounds nice and has an uplifting meaning, a name that you can be proud of, is not easy. The task is even more difficult when you are trying to find a name in a language that is not familiar to your surroundings.

For Indians living outside of India, finding a name for their baby becomes significantly more involved. Should you choose a name that is familiar to your local friends and colleagues? Would your child's non-Indian friends be able to pronounce that name? Would the child be able to pronounce the name? (You

65

may be surprised as to how many Indian kids say their own names with an accent). Does it have any other hidden meaning that may come back to haunt your child during his or her formative years?

To make your task a bit easier, we have compiled some pointers to keep in mind before selecting a name for your child:

**Meaning may be more important than you think**

Although we all recognize the importance of the meaning, we may not put enough emphasis on it. The impact the meaning of a name creates is astounding in a child's growth. It is amazing how a child feels brave or special or pretty or sweet in response to the meaning of her given name. So recognize the significance of the meaning while choosing a name for your baby.

**Emphasize proper pronunciation**

A name is only as good as it sounds — especially as said by the person who owns it. It is often distressing to see a child himself pronounce his or her name incorrectly. The other disadvantage of a hard-to-pronounce name is that it is likely to be shortened or altered by the child or others. Repeat the name hundreds of time to yourself, before selecting it. Have your friends at work, neighbors at home, your Indian friends, and young children, pronounce the name before selecting it to see how it sounds.

**Worry about the hidden meaning**

This can be a big problem. Often the slang meaning of a word that is similar to the name can create an abusive situation for your child at school or on the playground. Many beautiful Indian names fit into this category. Obvious ones are Nishit, Ishit, Aasman, Gopee, Anal and such. But there may be many not-so-obvious ones. So pay attention to the currency of that word.

**Think of the entire name (full name as will be written and said)**

Often it is easy to pick a name that meets all the criteria above but forget how the entire name would sound when it is put together. We have all heard such initials such as "P.K", "I.M." and "O.K." So think of the entire name and the initials it will make while selecting the name.

**Remember what you pick will stick**

Some names sound very good on a young boy or a girl but they may outgrow that name once they enter adulthood. Watch out for such names since the name you will pick today will be with that person forever.

**Worth repeating**

This has been said earlier but it is worth repeating. Please make sure that the child himself or herself learns the proper pronunciation of his or her name. I have seen so many young kids who cannot pronounce their own names. I find this to be highly disturbing. Insist on proper pronunciation of first and last name as much as possible.

# Language: The nourishing roots of any culture

The value of language cannot be over emphasized in imparting culture. In fact, language and culture both go hand in hand and a child, who does not know the language of her or his own heritage, will have a harder time grasping the nuances of the culture. Translations can hardly do full justice, but knowing the language will instantly put the child at an advantage in the culture.

If you and your partner speak two different languages, or come from two different parts of India, you may want to expose your child to both languages if you can. Experts say that a child can learn up to six languages without difficulty. Or you may choose to teach your child Hindi, India's national language.

Whichever language you decide upon, start early. You may not want to institute formal lessons, but let the child hear the language around her, let her soak it in; encourage him to talk in that language and, yes most importantly if he makes a mistake, do not laugh. Depending upon the age of your child, explain various words and their connection to Indian culture – whenever possible.

Knowing the language will also put your children instantly at ease while visiting India or when visitors from India come. The added benefit of this is that when they have an enjoyable visit, they are more likely to repeat that experience – especially when they are teenagers and can connect with their cousins.

Granted that in modern India, almost everyone – at least in large cities – speaks English, but even then, knowing the language will come in useful when talking and relating to those that do not.

Along with the spoken, colloquial language, teach the proper form also. Have at least one magazine or newspaper in your home that is in your language. That will help your child learn the language on his or her own.

**Some key words in English that share common roots with Sanskrit**

**Relations:**

Mother – matri,

Father – pitri,

Brother – bhratri

Daughter – duhitar

Name – naam

I am – Aham

Me – mai

Divine – deva

Saint – sant

**Body parts:**

Hand – hasta

Pedal – pada

Nose – nasika

Heart – hrit

Mind – mana

Dental- dant

# Songs and music: Dance your way to culture

Starting from when your children are very young, sing or play folk songs in any Indian language. There are so many musical tapes and CDs available of children's songs in almost every Indian language. These are songs that have catchy tunes – similar to nursery songs – and children will quickly pick up some of the words. Make it a habit to play or sing certain songs while giving them a bath, while putting them to sleep, or while you are preparing dinner. These habits will create strong memories and will help you turn down the TV for that segment of time.

Music provides a very strong yet latent learning experience for very young kids. The music that they hear will stay with them for a lifetime and evoke childhood feelings every time they hear it, even after they have grown up. In addition, children's songs use simple words and concepts that are a strong part of the culture where the music originates.

One note: although Hindi film music is popular among the Indian community, remember that it is often inappropriate, and has roots in a fantasy culture. Try to search for authentic children's songs. There will be time in the future for Hindi film music, but not when the children are very young.

# Etiquette and manners: Make your children "insiders"

> ▷ A friend of mine once commented that sometimes when
> we think we are being discriminated against, often
> it is not because of the color of our skin or our racial
> origins but because we do not understand the "right"
> protocol of the society we are living in. Social protocol,
> more than any other thing defines who the "insider" is.

> ▷ As a new immigrant to America, I was taken aback when
> I offered to lift some heavy files for an elderly co-worker
> and she told me quite sharply, that she was quite capable of
> managing on her own. I could not understand what was
> offensive about my offer to help. That experience taught me a
> lot about my lack of understanding about the society I was in.

> ▷ An American friend of mine, who is married to an Indian, told
> me this story: At the time of her wedding, she hugged all of her
> American family members and friends. When she stood before her
> husband's family members, she bent down to touch their feet – a
> normal custom during an Indian wedding. Her friends, who were
> unaware of this custom, thought that she had lost her balance.
> They rushed to help her get up only to be told that she was
> receiving blessings from family members by touching their feet.

Every culture has its own set of norms regarding what is acceptable and what is not. The difference between being an outsider and insider usually rests on an awareness and understanding of these norms or protocol. So, for anyone to feel comfortable and

71

enjoy the niceties of any culture, it is advantageous to know the etiquette of that culture.

Children growing up outside of India may need to be taught specific manners and behaviors that may come naturally to kids growing up within India. There is protocol to be observed within a home environment, in a community environment, and in public places such as temples. Teaching your children these basic manners will help them feel that they belong, and are not outsiders when they visit India or are in any Indian environment. Though some may be distinctly Indian, like touching the feet of elders on important days to receive their blessings, these manners are no different than those your child will be required to learn in America or anywhere in the world.

Simple things such as how you greet a friend, or an elderly relative, or a stranger, and table manners such as not using both hands while eating your food, or manners while visiting such as what it means to be a good guest, these are small but very important rules of protocol. Of course these rules vary from family to family and region to region. But as parents, you will want to make your kids aware of your family's etiquette and the customs and manners of others with whom they may visit, whether you are in an Indian home in America or on a visit to India.

Interestingly, as an added bonus, when a child understands and appreciates the niceties of one set of manners and culture, it also helps him or her to understand and value the manners and cultural nuances of other cultures including those of the western culture.

Teach your children a basic code of conduct in the Indian "way of life":

▷ How to greet elder people when you visit their home or when they come to visit your home.

▷ What to do when you enter any Indian household. (Take your shoes off, or at least ask if this is the family custom.)

▷ What to do while visiting a temple.

▷ What is the appropriate clothing for certain special occasions?

▷ How to approach a stranger during an Indian get-together.

▷ What is the proper way to eat Indian food?

▷ What is the proper way to serve Indian food?

▷ How does one show respect while visiting a family shrine?

You may think of many more that specifically apply to your own family or hometown. Make sure your children are exposed to these codes of conduct at a younger age since it will be harder to teach them, when they get older.

## Who is who in the family

One of the unique aspects of Indian families is that each relative has a special identifier title as a relative. In fact, it is so deeply ingrained in family life that there are songs to identify different relationships within a family. In the web of Indian family life, every member has a title that identifies how exactly he or she is related to each other. For example, *"kaka"* or *Chacha"* immediately communicates that one is the brother of the speaker's father. *Bua* in Hindi or *foi*, in Gujarati, signifies that a woman is your father's sister and *mausi* is your mother's sister. It may go a long way in instilling the culture if you teach your children to address each relative with his or her title instead of calling everyone by the generic uncle and auntie title. These titles reflect the beautiful aspect of Indian culture and it is easy to sustain because when young children are learning to speak it is easier to introduce these names. When the child gets used to referring to relatives in a certain way it might be harder to change later; so, like everything else, being aware of these nuances when the child is younger and willing to learn can go a long way.

## Clothes: Instilling a sense of what is appropriate

Just like the language you speak, the clothes you wear reflect who you really are. A child growing up in a family knows this intuitively. This does not mean you expect children to be dressed up all the time, but you do want to make them to be aware of proper clothing choices for any given certain situation and place. Doing so early on can create in them a respect for the culture. For example, just as a teenager would feel uncomfortable wearing a sari on the beach, she must recognize that wearing tank tops and shorts would be inappropriate in a temple or at a pooja. The issue is learning what is appropriate where and we want our children to develop a sense of appropriateness *before* they develop a negative attitude.

# 5

# *Everyday Life*

When I started writing this book, I first titled it "Everyday Ways to Give Culture to Your Children" because I really believe that culture is something that is imparted every moment, in the routine of your life. Little rituals go a long way. It is not how you celebrate Diwali or how you plan your trip to India that will make as much difference as how you live your everyday life. Small routines and rhythms of everyday life will impact your child much more than an occasional burst of cultural infusion. Here are some ways you can influence the environment in your home.

## Morning time

*A few days ago my college-bound daughter who was home for the holidays told me how she associates morning at home with certain music that we played every morning while she was home. To her, that was part of being at home.*

I think we all have very vivid memories of our childhood mornings. There are certain routines in every household that creates the environment that is unique to each family. Be it through some music, chanting, cooking a certain food, or a certain smell of incense. These are unique things to each household and their

75

own rhythm of life. Create an environment in your home that is consistent and uplifting. Here are some of the suggestions:

▷ Choose some soothing music, be it some chanting or light classical music, or devotional music and play it every morning.

▷ If possible, have a simple breakfast routine that allows everyone to be together for a few minutes in the morning. I know this is difficult as everyone is rushing to their jobs and schools, but even five minutes of cereal time or teatime might go a long way.

▷ Do you get a newspaper every morning? If so, having that lying around on the breakfast table may help children catch a glimpse of what is happening around them. Of course this is not applicable when children are under five years of age.

▷ Light a lamp and burn incense in the morning at your family altar soon after taking a shower. The fragrance of the incense will stay in your child's memory forever.

▷ Play the same radio station in the morning if anything from the above mentioned is a bit too much to include in your busy lives.

## Homework time

Although it is difficult to make homework time pleasurable, you can at least try to make it less painful by keeping a certain environment. Here are some of the things that may work for you:

▷ For young children (elementary school) working around the kitchen or a family room may make it more enjoyable as he or she can talk to an adult.

▷ Avoid watching TV while children are doing homework. It can be distracting for them.

▷ Play some music in the background.

▷ After dinner, if possible, try to work on your own paperwork or catch up on your reading while children are working on their homework. It helps create the environment of study that helps youngsters better focus on their studies.

▷ Discuss homework during dinnertime to help the children start thinking ahead, especially if it is a book report or a paper that needs to be written.

## Dinnertime

In the harried lifestyle we live, one of the first casualties can be dinnertime. Everyone is busy, the schedules are different, the TV is on and the phone is ringing. So many nights' dinners are eaten on the run, or in front of the TV screen. But we forget the high price in terms of health and happiness that is being paid when dinners are undermined. According to a recent article in *Organic Style Magazine* (October 2004), experts believe that having regular sit-down meals leads to better grades, half the risk of substance abuse, and makes children more likely to grow into well-adjusted adults. Besides, a lot can be gained when dinnertime is treated as special event. Treat your dinnertime as a sacred time for you and your family, and you will see the rewards right away.

**Pray before you eat**

Besides the obvious advantage of offering a prayer before we eat, it also gives a couple of minutes to quiet down before we begin. In Ayurveda it has been said that it is not only what you eat, but also when you eat, what kind of emotional state you are in when you eat, and whom you eat with that helps one digest their food better. So by doing a small prayer will help you calm down and see dinner as what it really is — a ritual, a common ritual creates a bond within a family.

**Offer food to the family deity**

This is similar to the point made earlier. Offering your food to the family deity can bring a sense of sacredness to your meals. In Hindu philosophy, food (anna) holds a sacred place. Treating food that is going to nourish you, with respect makes sense. This is especially important for young children to learn in times when their choice seems to rule on the dinner table.

**Turn off the TV turn on soft music**

Another obvious yet rarely practiced habit is to turn off the TV while eating dinner. If your household is one such household, practice it for a week and see how much difference it makes. You will find that everyone is paying attention to what they are eating. Even the dinnertime talk seems to take better shape when the environment is quiet. Tell everyone that dinner is a special time and you insist that it should be treated as such.

**Do not eat until hungry**

While this should be something natural and intuitive, we somehow "unlearn" this natural habit and eat at any odd time. One way to make sure that everyone is hungry at the time of dinner is to refrain from snacking at least one or two hours before dinnertime. With planning and discipline you and your family will reap good benefits from this habit and will be able to make dinnertime more pleasant.

**Wash hands before eating**

Another small but good habit is to make sure that everyone washes their hands before coming to dinner. Along with helping you getting rid of the germs and bacteria, this helps put the family into the clean mood to enjoy the food they are about to eat.

**Place fresh flowers or light candles on the table**

If possible, get fresh flowers for your dinner table. Often flowers from your own garden can do the job. They do not have to be a very expensive bouquet. Even a small bunch of fresh flowers can do the trick. If flowers are not practical in the dead of the winter, light a candle. Think about it. All day we work hard. A nice meal at the end of the day can make it all worth it.

**If you have a pet, feed him first**

It has been said that by offering your food to someone before you consume it, you are making a conscious choice of helping someone else. If you have a pet, feed him first. Teach your children to feed him before he or she comes to the dinner table.

**Refrain from eating standing up**

Sitting down to eat makes your meals special. It also helps if you are trying to lose weight. For your children, it will teach them to treat their food with respect and will make them aware of their eating habits.

**Select a topic of discussion for dinner**

For families with school-age children, this is a great option. Pre-assign topics such as current events for every Monday, science for Tuesdays and so on and make that a dinnertime topic. Let your children pick a topic of their choice. Be careful not to turn this into a one-sided lecture but make it a lively discussion. Be creative about these topics: music, entertainment, films, religion, and politics, family, health — the list can be endless.

**Refrain from criticizing the food**

This may be obvious but is worth mentioning. Criticism can happen without us realizing it if we are not consciously making the effort to eliminate it. I believe that out of respect to the person who has prepared the food and out of an understanding that there are so many in the world who go hungry every night, it is very important that young children learn to respect what is being offered on the table.

# Summertime

When the last day of school arrives, your children come home with their backpacks all excited and you wonder, "What will I do for the next two and half months with them that is enjoyable, educational, relaxing and engaging?" It is not easy! You want to use this time to be with your children and to make it a memorable summer for them. What can you do? Here are some suggestions:

▷ Try to at least spend two to three weeks with your children in a relaxed atmosphere.

▷ If possible, teach them one Indian language at home. If they are already learning an Indian language at a Sunday or other cultural school, either teach more of the same language or introduce them to another Indian language.

▷ Watch a few good family movies together — not as a way to keep them busy while you are doing other things but as a family activity. Make one night, say Thursday night, a movie night at your house and make it special.

▷ Read a classic book. Either pick a story like Ramayana or Mahabharat or read some other book, but enjoy reading together.

▷ Spread out a sheet in the backyard and observe the night sky together. Find a book on astronomy and look for the stars. There is something special about night sky that brings closeness to the family.

▷ Pull out a family album and identify various extended family members.

▷ Cook together. Depending upon their age, involve them in every aspect of cooking — from preparing the menu to serving. Kids love getting involved in the kitchen, especially the younger ones. It not only gives them something to do but also it shows them that they can eat their own creation and that is fascinating to them.

▷ Play games. Children love when parents are fully there with them and playing games is one way to assure your full presence. Of course in the days of cell phone and laptops, some parents try to "please" the child by playing games while also talking on the phone or working on the laptop.

## Car time

I once read a bumper sticker, which stated quite accurately: "If woman's place is in the kitchen, what am I doing in the car?"

It is true. As most parents know a lot of time is spent driving children around from one activity to another. In fact, this is often the most quality time parents have with their children. There are fewer distractions (cell phones have now invaded this time as well, but still TV and other distractions are less) and there is a close proximity that is invaluable. I found that this time was one of the best times to "communicate" with my children.

Here are a few suggestions:

**Share music**

On a long ride, take turns selecting and sharing music. I often found that music allowed me to talk about my "youth" days with my children. Of course, music is omnipresent when it comes to young children; it is the *kind* of music you select in the shared space of a car that may help create a bond.

**Make a conversation**

Somehow the close proximity of sitting in a car seems to be conducive to talking about often tough subjects. If you find that your child is trying to talk to you about something, pay attention and take advantage of the time together. One note to parents: refrain from giving long lectures and engage in a real conversation (with talking and listening). A note: if you find that the topic of conversation can turn into an argument, avoid talking at that time and find a special time at home when you can talk about the subject without distractions of traffic.

**Play games**

On long rides, different games from Antakshari to Memory can be a great way to enjoy and share. Identify different cars on the road, look at their license plates, and talk about the different states that they are from; you can also talk about different carmakers and where they are located.

# Nighttime

Just as morning time, nighttime is also a very special time in a family and creates strong memories for young children. Of course many of the suggestions here are similar to the morning routine but the difference can be in the kind of pace you create through these traditions. Most parents have a special routine for tucking their children to bed; here are a few suggestions that will add cultural flavor:

**Pray**

Most families have a routine of some sort that involves prayer before bed for young children, but it is worth mentioning just in case it has not been part of your routine already.

**Read a book**

Again, although this is an obvious and familiar activity to most parents, the innovative selection of a book every night can make a big difference. There are books that help your child sleep better such as *Moonbeam: A book of meditation for children* or stories about Krishna and Rama that can add the cultural dimension you desire.

**Tell a story**

If you are good with the art of storytelling, you have an excellent opportunity to tell your children stories from your past. Young children enjoy hearing about their parents "own" stories, if they are told with a flare.

**Breathing exercise**

There are simple visualization techniques that can help children relax better before going to sleep. You can create your own simple routine of counting breaths and visualizing your child's favorite things as you lull her to sleep.

## Music

Of course soothing music is a universally known and accepted way to drift into sleep. Select and play a well-suited "dhun" or mantra chanting music each night.

# *Festivals and Celebrations*

❖

> *Through our children, we live twice.*

Festivals, just like folk songs, reflect the true essence and are an honest mirror of any culture. While religious leaders and scholars may argue about the intricacies of a culture, and experts may write huge philosophical books to describe a culture, but people, who live their everyday lives by unseen threads of culture, exhibit those values through festivals. Festivals are the living and breathing display of any culture.

Festivals are also a way to stop the busy lives we live to reflect, to meet others, to spend time with our family members, to create memories for the younger generation and to delve into family stories! No wonder festivals are the best part of any culture.

But festivals are community events so to celebrate any festival we need an environment, an environment that can only be created by having the entire community celebrate the festival. In the absence of the community, celebrating a festival is not impossible, but you have to try harder, you have to be more creative, and you have to plan ahead.

Of course every festival is celebrated differently and in the following pages you will read about some major Indian festivals, what they are, the story behind them, how they are celebrated, when they typically fall in a year and practical tips to celebrate them at home.

But before we get to each festival and its specific details, here are some general suggestions for you to consider when it comes to celebrating Indian festivals in your home:

### "Adopt" a festival

In the busy lives we live when we have young children, it may be difficult to celebrate every festival in its full glory. Instead "adopt" one festival out of so many festivals and celebrate it every year. If you have a group of friends or family who can pick different holidays, children may benefit from learning about more holidays without too much stress on parents.

### Encourage friends to adopt different festivals

Often big festivals like Diwali may mean several invitations to parties and celebrations while another festival, such as Holi may go without celebration at all. Talk to your friends to see if you all can take turns hosting the different holidays.

### Create memories

Do something special that is memorable for children under age ten. This will create a strong memory and an identification with that festival. Be creative and include a craft or art activity or involve kids in preparing a special meal or decorating the family shrine.

### Tell stories

Find colorful stories for each festival and tell the story. If possible, get a nice, age appropriate, book with pictures that tell the story. For children stories make a wonderful connection and engage their imagination.

**Create a small "holiday" library in your home**

For each festival collect nice books and create a special holiday library. A small bookcase named "holiday" or some such creative way to identify it as a special library will make children think about finding a book whenever there is a holiday.

**Take kids to India during a holiday**

(This suggestion actually came from my daughter who reminded me that once she was about the age of nine, we had taken her to India during Diwali time. She said that she really enjoyed celebrating Diwali in an authentic atmosphere). While children are young enough to take time off from school, and yet old enough to remember (around the ages of nine to fourteen), pick a festival and make a family trip to India during that time. Seeing and participating in a festival celebration when everyone around you is immersed in the celebration creates a much stronger impression in young minds.

While the above tips are useful for celebrating any Indian festival in your home, the following suggestions and tips are to help you show how to celebrate some important festivals from India in America. I have tried to give the significance of the festival as well as various ways you can make them part of your busy lives – especially with young children. Obviously there are many more ways to celebrate these festivals and many of you may have already created a better way to celebrate them. The ideas here are just some to jump-start your creativity and imagination.

# Diwali

*While our daughters were younger, we tried a special way to celebrate Diwali. We would have an Open House from 2 pm and scheduled every hour with an activity. Since guests knew this ahead of time, they could pick the time of their favorite activity. Activities included making rangoli on wood planks that can be taken home, henna design while we played some Diwali music in the background, having someone tell a story about Diwali, clay pot Diya making, or candle making followed by aarti and dinner. Though this Diwali open house started as a small gathering of close friends, soon the word spread and we were delighted to see it grow exponentially.*

Diwali is one of the most celebrated Hindu festivals around the world. There are several stories associated with the five days of Diwali celebrations. One of the most familiar is the story of Rama's victory and return to his kingdom. The other story associated with Diwali is of Narakasur. But above all, Diwali is a festival of lights and it falls on one of the darkest nights. Diwali — the five-day festival — falls on the last four days of the Hindu month Ashwin. (The fifth day is the new-year day for the people who follow the Vikram Samvat calendar).

The celebration of Diwali includes Laxmi Pooja, lots of firecrackers, a variety of food, meeting everyone in the community, decorating houses with oil lamps and rangoli design, visiting temples, closing of the accounting books (for the merchant community), new clothes, and long holidays.

Here are some of the ways to celebrate Diwali with your friends and other family members:

# How to make Diwali memorable for your children

## Think activities

Children enjoy doing activities. Include one or several activities related to Diwali depending upon the age of the children. Rangoli making with colored rice or colored powder, making designs on pre-made Diya holders, candle making, and aarti plate decorations are a few of the activities that you can creatively include in your party. Even adults have fun taking part in such activities.

## Tell a story or read a book

If you know someone who is a good storyteller, you are in luck. This may be a great opportunity to involve a grandparent or an elderly member within the community. Have Grandma or Grandpa prepare a story or a couple of stories that can be told with flair. If you cannot find anyone, look for a well-written book that is age appropriate and find a person who can read it aloud. There are many books on Diwali available in the market today. (You can try *Here Comes Diwali*: The Festival of Lights published by MeeRa Publications, publishers of this book).

## Cook something together

Think of a recipe where you can involve children. It would be wonderful if you can think of an item that is cooked traditionally around Diwali time in your home. Can you involve them in kneading, decorating, or something similar? Children love making something special and then enjoy savoring them. You may also make this as a take-home treat for them and their friends.

### Sing and dance

One note of caution: avoid staged performance. Instead think of any folk music and dancing that can involve everyone. Although specific Diwali-related music might be hard to find, you may use some folk songs and music to create the festive mood.

### Invite non-Indian friends or family

Invite a few non-Indian friends, preferably with similar age children, on the actual Diwali day and introduce them to a Diwali celebration. You may include small pooja or aarti, as part of the celebration if you so choose. Teaching their non-Indian friends about their culture may be the best way for your children to learn it for themselves.

### Play

A game like Jeopardy or a guessing game where simple questions about Diwali can be asked may be a great way to provide fun and education at the same time. You may include this as a part of storytelling hour or keep it as a separate activity.

### Involve grown-ups

Ask everyone in the party to share their memories about the best Diwali they ever had. Find out what kind of things stick in their memory and why. Also ask everyone to describe how Diwali was celebrated in his or her families back in India. Or alternatively, have a large floor rangoli design where all the grown-ups can fill colors.

### Treat the whole class

Bring special sweets to your child's class and have him or her share it with the classmates. Bring slides or a video showing celebrations. Bring and read a book to the children. If possible, let your child explain to her classmates what Diwali is all about.

**Fireworks**

If you are living in a state where fireworks are permitted, you have a great opportunity to make your party memorable. Find safe fireworks and make them the highlight of your evening. I know one family that will light fireworks even if there is snow in the yard on Diwali day!

**Avoid a regular party**

There is no better way to bore young children then to take them to a regular grown-up party where it is hard to distinguish what is special about Diwali.

**Light a lamp**

Light a lamp at the family shrine, preferably in the morning after taking a shower, but also anytime during the day is fine. If you have pre-made wicks, lighting the lamp will only take a couple of minutes in the morning. If you can use "ghee" it is good, otherwise use oil, but the actual act of lighting the "diya" will supplement the mental celebration of Diwali. If you have incense sticks, this is a perfect time to use them as well.

**Rangoli or Aum on the threshold**

Creating a small design on a wooden plank or on your front porch will create an environment of celebration. Alternatively, take a vermilion paste and put a design on the important thresholds inside your home.

**Candles on the windowsill**

Put a few candles on the windowsill of your home or apartment during all five days of Diwali. I remember attending a professional seminar once around October and the seminar leader asked me if there was a special festival that had just passed. I told her it was Diwali. She said that she lives in a neighborhood where there are several Indian families and during the past few days she had seen candles in several windows. Candles add to the festive mood around the house and help create the environment.

**Seek blessings**

If you are lucky enough to have an elderly relative living in close proximity, make it a point to visit them to seek their blessings. If possible, try to visit the temple at least once during the five-day Diwali time.

**Offer special treats to the family deity before eating**

During the five days of Diwali, offer your dinner plate to the family deity before sitting down to eat. Like many of the things suggested here, they are good habits to practice every day, but even introducing the ritual during Diwali is a good idea.

# Rakshabandhan (Rakhi)

Rakshabandhan or Rakhi, or Balev — as it is called in Gujarat — is a very special day for brothers and sisters. It is the day on which sister ties a thread on the wrist of her brother as a token of her love to protect him from the evil powers. Historically Rakhi was tied to protect brothers from war-related injuries. Rakshabandhan invokes a very special bond between brothers and sisters. On this day, Brahmins also change their Yagnopavit or the sacred thread after doing a special prayer.

Sisters usually recite the following sloka while tying the thread (Rakhi) to the brother.

*Yena baddho Balee raajaa daanavendro mahaabalah*
*Tena twaam anubadhnaami rakshe maa chala maa chala*

*"I am tying a Raksha (Rakhi) to you, similar to the one tied to Bali, the powerful and generous king.*
*Oh Raksha, be firm, do not go away, do not go away."*

Various parts of India celebrate Rakshabandhan differently. Across Northern India and many other sections, tying Rakhi to one's brother and offering him protection is a way to celebrate Raksha Bandhan. In Maharashtra this day is called Narial Purnima or Coconut Full Moon Day. On this day, the people of Maharashtra, offer coconuts to the Sea God Varuna, as a form of worship.

In Southern India, Rakshabandhan is called Avani Avittam and on this day Brahmins wear a new sacred thread, recite Vedas, and offer their prayers.

Rakshabandhan falls on the full-moon day of the month of Shravan in a Hindu calendar.

# Celebrating Raskhabandhan at home:

Here are some of the special ways to celebrate Rakhi in your home.

**Make your own Rakhi**

Many art supply stores carry several little items that can be used to make your own Rakhi. If you have the time, inclination, and inspiration, make various kinds of Rakhi with your children. How about a nice "friendship" bracelet? Young children will have fun and feel proud to share their creations with their peers.

**Cook a special meal**

Involve young sisters to cook something special for their brothers. Try making some simple sweet with them. On the day of

Rakshabandhan make a special meal and offer it to the family deity before eating.

**Make a special Pooja Thali**

Take any large plate and create a small design with Kumkum powder or any other colored powder. Add a nice oil lamp in the middle and a place to hold Rakhi. Make it a special time for brothers and sisters.

**Make a Rakshabandhan card**

How about making a nice card for the brother? Get some construction paper and crayon out and make a card together with your daughter.

**Talk about the special bond between brothers and sisters**

Take this opportunity, especially for slightly older children, to explain the special relationship between brothers and sisters. There are several stories in Hindu mythology about brothers and sisters. If you know any such story, share it with your children.

Note: If you do not have immediate family members nearby you can celebrate Rakshabandhan with friends and their children.

# Navratri/Durga Pooja

Navratri — which literally translates as "nine nights" — is a very unique festival of India. It is the festival when the feminine power is worshipped for nine days in all different forms: as a giver of knowledge (Saraswati), as a giver of prosperity (Laxmi), as a nurturing power (Amba), and as a ferocious destroyer of evils in the world (Durga). Navratri usually falls in October. According to the Indian calendar Navratri — or the nine nights – are the first nine days of the waxing moon during the month of Ashwin.

Like many other festivals of India, Navratri is celebrated differently in different parts of India. The interesting part, however, is that the key notion behind all these various celebrations remains the same — worshipping the female power of fertility, education, prosperity, and protection. One of the main festivities that Navratri is known for is the folk dance of Gujarat and Rajasthan. Almost all communities in U.S. and Canada now celebrate Navratri by organizing dances. So, of course, the best way to introduce young children to Navratri is by participating in this community event. However, here is how you can bring the spirit of Navratri in your home as well.

▷ Visit at least one Garba/Dandia Raas event. Teach steps of the dance to your children.

▷ Visit a temple where Havan is being performed or if possible, perform a Havan at home.

▷ Make or visit a home where Kolu — steps of wooden planks decorated with different themes by young girls and their mothers in Southern India in praise of Goddess Saraswati, the goddess of knowledge — is arranged.

▷ Have a small prayer at home to pay respect to Goddess Saraswati. Have your children bring their books to the prayer room and put them next to the Goddess statue or a picture, to be blessed by the Goddess.

▷ Since the tenth day of Navratri is Dusserra — the day on which thousands of years ago Sri Rama killed the evil king Ravana — many communities celebrate Ravan Dahan or burning of the statue of Ravana. If possible, take your children to such an event. Tell the story of Sri Rama and his battle with Ravana.

▷ Share your childhood story about Navratri; what you did as a child during Navratri, what you enjoyed the most, etc. can fuel a lot of questions from a young child at bedtime.

▷ Get a special dress for your child for Garba. Gift your child with Dandia sticks.

▷ Attend a Durga Pooja in your community with your children. (See below).

**Durga pooja**

In Bengal, Durga Pooja, a celebration of Goddess Durga takes place at the same time as Navratri. Durga pooja is a highly celebrated festival where devotees perform homa (havan), offer specially made food to Durga and invite friends and family members to join in the celebration.

# Janmashtami

Janmashtami literally means "birth on the eighth day." Krishna – one of the most popular Gods of Hindu, who was an incarnation of God Vishnu - was born to Devki and Vasudev on the dark night of Shravan's eighth day, so Janmashtami is celebrated at midnight (the exact time of Krishna's birth) of that day. Janmashtami usually falls in the month of August. Since the birth of Krishna is at midnight, children are excited to be allowed to stay up late. The day of the birth of Krishna is celebrated joyously throughout communities. Here is how you can celebrate it at home:

▷ Decorate your family shrine and a statue of Krishna with fresh flowers, nice clothes and jewelry.

▷ Make special sweets to be distributed at midnight.

▷ Have confetti or flower petals ready to throw on the statue of Krishna at midnight.

▷ Learn a new Krishna bhajan with your family.

▷ Sing songs or tell stories about Krishna until midnight.

▷ Read a book about Krishna with your family.

# Holi

Holi is one of most fun-filled and colorful festivals since it crosses all the boundaries of age, gender, religion and economic status. It is the festival welcoming spring. Here are a few suggestions to celebrate Holi in your home or community.

**Read a book about Holi**

Holi is the story of Prahlad and his father King Hirnakasypu. Find a book about their story and read it to your children or their class. *Here Comes Holi: The Festival of Colors* published by MeeRa Publications offers a story of Prahlad and his father that you can read to your child.

**Splash colored powder, rice, or water**

If the weather is nice, invite your child's friends and let them play with colored water with their water guns or colored powder. Let the non-Indian friends know what Holi is and ask them to bring an extra pair of clothing to change into after the play is over. If the weather is not very nice make it a special day to color their favorite picture.

### Listen to Holi music

Holi is one festival that offers an array of music. Since Holi is attributed to Krishna and Radha, their playful love songs dominate the airways in India during Holi. Play the music at home to create an environment of celebration.

### Light a small bonfire

If possible, at dusk light a small bonfire in your backyard or porch. Tell the story of Prahlad and his Aunt Holika.

### Color a picture of Krishna and Radha

Krishna and Radha are depicted in almost all the Holi stories and pictures. Find a nice picture of Krishna and Radha and color it with young children.

### Make a special meal

In many parts of India, on the day Holi people eat popcorn and dates. In the evening they prepare a special meal to celebrate Holi. So, if possible, make something special for dinner to mark the fun celebration of Holi.

# Onam

### The story

Onam celebrates the golden age of King Mahabali. King Mahabali was a noble king of Asura dynasty. However, a feeling of superiority marred his nobility. As the story goes, God Vishnu (who loved King Mahabali) wanted to relieve him of the load of superiority, which can be destructive. Hence he incarnated as Vamana (a dwarf) and approached the king when the latter was performing "Maha Yagna" to affirm his superiority over the three worlds. When the king asked him what he wanted, Vamana said he wanted just three feet of land. The king laughed but when he asked Vamana to measure the land, Vamana grew and he covered the entire earth with one foot, the sky with his other foot and then asked the king where could he place his third step. The king now understood that he was not dealing with a dwarf, realized his own boastful arrogance and offered his own head to the god to take his third step. Vishnu stepped on the king's head, who at once was enlightened with wisdom and liberated to merge with the divine. God Vishnu was very pleased with the humility of the king and granted him the reward of visiting his home state once a year on the day of Onam.

Onam is celebrated for ten days, during which time everyone puts a flower mat in front of their homes to welcome the king and the god.

Here is what you will see if you were to visit the state of Kerala during Onam:

▷ Snake boat races

▷ The flower mats in front of homes

▷ Kathakali dances in the community

▷ Delicious gourmet food with several tasteful delicacies shared with family and friends on the fourth day of Onam.

Here is what you can do to celebrate Onam at home:

▷ Make and put flower mats in front of the house.

▷ On fourth day of Onam, prepare a gourmet lunch or dinner for the entire family.

▷ If possible, invite friends for dinner.

# Pongal

Pongal falls on January 13 to January 16 of each year and since it follows the solar calendar, unlike many other festivals, it always falls on the same dates.

Pongal is the first festival of each New Year in the Indian state of Tamil Nadu. Each day of this festival has a special significance; however, it is celebrated more grandly in the villages, while the city folk mainly celebrate on the second day only.

The first day of the festival is called *Bhogi*. On Bhogi all people clean out their homes from top to bottom, and collect all unwanted goods. In the evening, people will light bonfires and burn whatever can be burnt. In villages where people live in mud huts with thatched roves, the porches of the homes are taken apart and reconstructed along with the front section of the walkway in front of their homes.

The second day of the festival, *Surya Pongal*, is the day on which the celebrations actually begin, and it is the first day of the Tamil month Thai. On this day Surya, the sun God, is worshipped and people wake early to create elaborate kolum – colored rice-flour paste design — on the ground in front of their doorway or home. People wear their new dresses and use new utensils. Also on this day the new rice is collected and cooked in pots until they overflow. The word Pongal means overflowing. This overflowing of rice is a joyous occasion, and the children and adults as well will shout out "Pongal-o Pongal!" Children will dance and make music to the tune of these words. The rice is cooked and prepared as a dish called Pongal, made with rice, dhal and sugar.

The third day is called *Maatu Pongal*. This day is devoted to paying homage to cattle. Cows and bulls are decorated with paint and bells and people pray to them. Kumkum (red vermillion) is placed on their head, and people pay respect to them by bending down, like praying in temple, and touching their feet and foreheads, followed by an aarthi and offering the cattle prasaad (food offering, in this case, pongal). In some villages in South India, there are bullfights of varying types.

The fourth day is known as *Kaanum Pongal*. On this day, people travel to see other family members. Younger members of the family pay homage to the elders, and the elders thank them by giving small amounts of money. People also leave some food out on banana leaves for birds to take.

So Pongal is really a celebration of families, relatives, friends, animals, birds, and the entire creation.

Although it is not possible to celebrate this fully outside of India, here we can at least do a few things so that children remember the holiday.

▷ Make pongal and other special treats for the family and friends.

▷ Clean the house.

▷ Buy new clothes.

▷ Pray together as a family.

▷ Offer a special treat to your pet, if you have one.

▷ Put birdseeds in your backyard.

# Yugadi

Yugadi is a celebration of a new year (Samvatsara) as per the Hindu calendar. It usually falls in the month of April. It is signified by the earth's rotation around the Sun each year representing one complete cycle. Each beginning of a new cycle is the day of Yugadi. It also represents a new beginning for all efforts. It is believed that however one spends that day will influence the forth-coming year. Thus everyone should spend that day in peace and joy through spiritual, religious and cultural activities.

Here are some of the activities that are observed on this festival:

▷ Special bath

▷ Home decoration

▷ Making new resolutions (Taking oath)

▷ Offering Pooja and special prayers

▷ Homa (Havan)

▷ Reading of Panchanga (traditional Hindu Calendar)

▷ Charity and donation

▷ Special prasad of neem leaves and jaggery

# Makarsakranti or Lohri

This is another Indian festival that follows the Christian calendar. It falls on January 14, of every year, the day when according to Hindu astronomy the sun enters the rashi (zodiac) of Makara

(Capricorn). It is usually in the Hindu month of Posh or Magh. The day is also called Uttarayan because the Sun is now entering the northern journey as the day becomes longer and the nights become shorter.

In different parts of India, this day is celebrated differently. For example, in Himachal Pradesh, Haryana, and Punjab it is called Lohri and is celebrated by a bonfire and a special meal. In Uttar Pradesh, it is called Khichdi. There is a great significance attached to charity and religious ceremonies. In the western states of Gujarat and Rajasthan, the day is celebrated as a kite flying day. The sky is filled with different colored kites during the day as everyone enjoys being on the terrace. At night, paper lanterns are tied to the kite strings making the entire sky look festive. There is also a big significance of Til (sesame seeds) during the festival. All parts of India people make something from sesame seeds — usually round sweet balls called Laddoo — and people add sesame seeds to their bath water. People eat special sesame candy and celebrate with the newly-harvested wheat recipes.

**How to celebrate Makarsakranti at home in America**

Since the celebration of Makarsakranti is dependent upon good weather, which is not practical in most part of America during the month of January, celebrating Makarsakranti at home can be difficult. However, the festival can be recognized by some of the following activities at home:

▷ Make sesame candy (sesame seed Laddoo) and offer it to your family deity as prasaad.

▷ If possible, visit a nearby temple with your children on that day.

▷ Change the sacred thread at your family shrine or in the community temple if you are wearing one.

Note: For many of these festivals, celebrating outside of India is limited. But you can at least make some mention of the festival and try to do something special, however, your children will at least become familiar with the holiday. The best thing you can do, when you get a chance, is to take your children to India during the time of any of these festivals where they are celebrated in their full form. The memory of such trips will remain in their minds for a long time.

# Ram Navmi

Ram Navmi, the birthday of Rama — who is also the reincarnation of Vishnu - falls on the ninth day of the Indian month Chaitra. It usually falls in March or April in the Western calendar. People celebrate it by doing prayers to Rama and chanting bhajan in temples and homes. Here are some of the things you can do to celebrate Ram Navmi in your home.

▷ Read Ramayana with your family members.

▷ Talk about Sri Rama and his life during dinnertime.

▷ Tell the story of Sri Rama.

▷ Make a special sweet and offer it to Lord Rama before dinner.

▷ Visit a nearby temple.

▷ Watch *Ramayana* available on video.

# Special Vrat

If you are in India — it feels like any day of the year — there is some special Vrat or pooja going on. The culture is filled with various ways to "praise" different Gods and Goddesses, finding different reasons to perform a pooja of their choice. Be it a new home, someone's special birthday, a new arrival in the family, full moon day, 11$^{th}$day of the lunar cycle called ekadashi and many others. Then there are young girls observing special fasting on various days from "Gauri vrat", married women observing "Vat Savitri Vrat", and many others observing fasting one day of the week of their choice. There is a Vrat to please "Vaibhav Lakshmi" and there is a Vrat to please "Santoshi Ma". There are celebrations when people complete the prescribed number of such "Vrat".

**What is Vrat?**

Vrat is a way to observe a particular day with prescribed food to eat or to avoid, special invocation to a particular or God or Goddess, and to do a special pooja. Although living outside of India it is not very common but as the community grows and puts down roots in the American soil, you may find more of these religious observations.

# Indian national holidays

In addition to these religious holidays, there are Indian national holidays that you may want to observe at your home, or in your community with your children. Here are some of the major ones.

# Independence Day of India and Republic Day of India

After one hundred and fifty years of British rule, India finally got its freedom on August 15, 1947. It is celebrated widely in India where it is also a national holiday. Here are a few things you can do to celebrate it outside of India:

▷ Take this opportunity to teach your children India's national anthem and its meaning.

▷ Display the Indian flag in your house.

▷ Buy or bake a cake decorated with "Happy Birthday India" in the colors of the flag, and share it with your friends, family, and colleagues.

▷ Pull out a map of India and take the opportunity to familiarize young children with it.

▷ Sing or play India's national anthem in the morning or prior to dinner with your family.

▷ Watch the movie *Gandhi* or any other movie about India's struggle for independence.

▷ With older children, talk about the freedom struggle. Tell them stories of Bhagat Singh, Netaji Subhashchandra Bose, and Rabindranath Tagore.

▷ Talk about the National Anthem and how it was selected.

▷ For small children, have them color the national flag of India.

# Celebrating birthdays

Once, someone asked a child when his birthday was so the child gave a date. The grown-up asked which year and the child, confused, replied, "What do you mean? Every year!"

Every parent knows that birthdays are very special to young children. In fact, that is the first date that they will remember. So what better opportunity than to inject the cultural aspect to this very important day? Here is a chance to create a tradition, to introduce an idea, to be creative. Do not let this wonderful opportunity get lost in the chaos of parties and gifts.

Here are some of the things you can do to celebrate your child's birthday:

**Prayers**

Make it a tradition to offer a prayer on a birthday. Have the child prepare a prayer, (e.g, sloka, bhajan) or just a few words to offer at the family shrine. No matter how busy your household is, try to have a small prayer with all the family members present, on everyone's birthday. This creates a tradition that your children will remember throughout their lives. This will also give you an opportunity to teach them the custom of asking for blessings from God as well as from grown-ups. Young children are usually so excited about their birthdays that they are willing to wake up early enough for you to accommodate a small prayer time in the morning. Take advantage of their enthusiasm to celebrate.

**Blow out candles or light a lamp?**

Did you know where the tradition of blowing candles on birthdays came from? According to one account this tradition — like giving a diamond ring — comes from marketing. When Kodak Camera Company wanted to promote taking pictures for birthdays, some marketing genius came up with the idea of blowing out a candle — to mark a Kodak moment.

Hindus believe that a life is like a light and when the life is gone we blow out a flame. On the other hand, it is a western tradition to blow out candles on one's birthday. So talk to your child — and her friends, if having a party — that your family's tradition is to light a candle instead.

If your child feels uncomfortable to do the opposite of the American tradition, at least light a Diya at home to mark his or her birthday.

## Downplay the idea of gifts

Although it is difficult in this day and age to completely stay away from gift giving on birthdays, at least you can downplay the whole process by highlighting other aspects of the birthday. Typically when friends or relatives call to wish Happy Birthday to a child, the second question they ask, (after, "How old are you now,") is "What did you get for your birthday?" Without realizing, these kinds of questions reinforce associating gifts with birthdays. Instead, try asking something like "So, what do you think you have learned in the past year?" or "How much do you think you have grown in the last year?" or something about the New Year.

## Donate something on behalf of your child

Talk to your child about the value of giving and how lucky he or she is when there are so many unfortunate kids in the world. See if you can involve your child in giving something of value to a good cause — even if it means something as small as sending candy to a homeless shelter. It is a good idea to show how making others happy can make you happy as well. Let your child select a person or a charity.

**Visit a museum**

Along with other things that you do on your child's birthday ask her to select a museum that she would like to go to. If you live close to a large city, you may have ample choices. You may decide to make this visit prior to the actual birthday or soon after and make it a special treat for the child. The memory will go a long way when it is associated with a birthday.

**Put Aum on the birthday cake**

While you are decorating the cake with "Happy Birthday" writing, see if you can add the symbol of AUM on the top.

# The Holiday season of America

The holiday season in America, from late November to late December is a fun time that envelops every household in America – or at least it feels like it. As much as these holidays are enjoyable and most Indian families have adopted them as their own to varying degrees, these holidays pose a challenge — as well as an opportunity — to Indian families. Each family can decide how much to adopt to make it special for their own family. The solution may be different in each household. But it may be important to keep in mind that after all, these are family times and you can make it special as just that with some special activity.

Here are some suggestions to see how we can make this time a great family time. (The ideas suggested here can also be used in another country while their holiday season is going on.)[1]

## How to make the holidays a family time

One of the best things about the holiday season is that it allows us to connect with our families and friends; but this is not easy. Often we are so rushed that we do not take time to make these visits memorable. Although we believe that once we are with our families, quality time will automatically happen, experience teaches us that we need to be aware of family dynamics and work to attain quality time. It is hard, but the rewards are immense. This holiday season, make your family your first priority. Plan ahead for any activity that you might enjoy together. Here are a few ways to make sure that you make your holidays special:

## Make a family tree

If your family involves a couple of generations and different sets of relatives, bring them all together to create a family tree. You can use a large piece of canvas or one of many software programs on the market. This activity will help jog the memories

---

[1] Many parents have shared their views about celebrating Christmas in their homes. A good majority of people seems to believe that since it is a religious holiday for Christians, non-Christians have no reason to celebrate it. Others have suggested that since everyone else is celebrating it, it may be a good idea to celebrate it within your home so your child does not feel left out. Some parents have come up with creative ways to have a Christmas tree but they decorate it with pictures of Hindu Gods and Goddesses. Whatever your views, here are some suggestions that can help you maximize this family time. After all, any holiday celebration boils down to creating memories and having a quiet and enjoyable time with family and friends.

of many older relatives. You can also combine this activity with sharing old pictures.

**Play games**

Board games can be an ideal way to perk up a lazy afternoon or an evening after a heavy dinner — especially when different age groups are together.

**Collect recipes from various members of your family**

If your family members are automatically attracted to the kitchen, use this time to ask them about their favorite recipes. You can ask them ahead of time to bring the recipe so that with a little bit of work it can turn into a family cookbook.

**Cook together**

One variation of the previous idea is to cook together if your kitchen is big enough and if it is an activity that family members will enjoy.

**Share family stories (or even secrets!)**

Every family has special stories. Have everyone share a story. It will be amazing to find out how much we do not know about our own family's history.

**Take a trip together**

Long weekends are perfect times to take a trip together with family members. Take a cruise or go to a resort place; alternatively visit a museum and enjoy a day outside. Often a new setting brings out a new side in everyone.

**Discuss a book**

If many members of your family enjoy reading, select a book and have everyone read that ahead of time. Or find a book that everyone has read. If you like the activity, you can choose the book many months in advance for next year's holiday season.

**Enjoy music together**

Have you come across some good music lately that you would like everyone to enjoy as well? Have different family members bring their favorite CD to share.

**Create a talent show**

If your family is full of talented people, have everyone prepare and present one item on a special evening. You can also make it a children's talent evening.

7

# India: Your Golden Opportunity

## Visiting India

> "I feel like one of the best things my parents did in teaching me Indian culture was to take me to India frequently. I have felt the warmth and beauty of the culture during those visits and was able to understand my own background better."

Taking your children to India is like giving them an intense course in the culture and family life of India. It can be overwhelming to both parents as well as children. Here are some things to do before you leave and while you are there to take full advantage of the intensity that such trips offer. If your New Year's plans include taking a trip to India, please consider the following points to make your trip culturally rewarding:

**Keep a positive attitude**

Children sense your attitude, and if they hear you make slight remarks about anything (the dirt, or filth, or the poverty in India) they will inherit those notions. Instead, let them notice you finding good and pointing out the hidden beauty of the culture, they too will begin to appreciate these qualities.

### Point out the positives

Along the same lines, try to show how even people who live in poverty can help others, or how your relatives show they care. India offers an abundance of opportunities to notice love and caring. Point out to your children something as simple as the ease with which you can visit a relative or friend there.

### Study a map of India before you go with your child

Depending upon the age of your child or children, it may be a good idea to study the map of India and to point out the areas you might be visiting. This can be a good starting point for conversations about India.

### Draw a map of India

You can take this as an arts and craft project with your children and draw or color India's map. Of course, like any other activity here, the goal is to talk about India and create the connection in a child's mind and heart.

### Visit a local school

If possible try to visit your local school or have your child attend a few days of school there. Try to talk with the teacher beforehand. (It can backfire if your child's experience is not positive.) Also, consider taking a gift that the entire class can use or enjoy.

### Gifts for the needy

Encourage your children to take gifts for the "unknown" poor kids in India and let them choose who they want to give the gift to. One note of caution: Unfortunately, to a child or any first time visitor, the poverty in India can be a jarring, shocking experience. Tactfully bring out that we can only do our share to help so that your child does not feel too overwhelmed by it.

**Look at a family album**

Before going, pull out a family album and identify the family members you will be meeting during your trip. This helps children get involved and feel less uncomfortable meeting "strangers."

**Have your child take pictures**

Buy an inexpensive camera that your child can use. Let him take pictures of what he finds important or interesting. Make an album and have him share with classmates after returning to the U.S.

**Celebrating festivals**

If possible plan your trip around an important Indian holiday. This may not be that difficult, as the Indian calendar is full of festivals. Some suggestions are: Uttarayan, Holi, Navraatri, Rakshabandhan. Try reading or talking about the holiday beforehand. If you plan to visit India during Diwali time, keep in mind that the constant sound of firecrackers may frighten young children. Consider warning them about the noise before leaving.

**Historical significance**

India is full of history. Take advantage of that and talk about the historical significance of the places you might be visiting. How old is the city? Who built it? Which is the oldest building? Such historical information will help a child see things in perspective and remember it for a long time.

# Visitors from India

One of the advantages of globalization is that travel between India and America has become a common occurrence. If you have any connection to India, you will receive many guests from India. Guests who may be your direct relative, your cousin, your friends, your cousin's cousins, your friend's friends, your friend's cousins and your cousin's friends! While it can get tiring to entertain guests, they offer a very unique opportunity to bring India closer to your children. Guests from India offer a very special glimpse for your children to interact with someone from a different background. Take this opportunity to further your goal of teaching cultural aspects:

**Suggest to your guest to talk in his or her own language if you can**

English is becoming a very common language in India now but, if possible, try to talk in Hindi or the mother tongue of your guest. This may not be practical if you do not know the language yourself but it will offer an opportunity to your child to experience another language.

**Show connections**

I remember a visit from my distant — very distant — cousin once who was attending a conference in Boston. It was wonderful to really trace our connections while the kids tried to figure out how exactly we were related! Young kids approach this like a puzzle to be solved or a challenge of their skill. Use this opportunity to talk about how you are related or how you know this person. Did you meet him in your college? How is she your cousin?

**A window into the past**

At the dinner table have your guest tell your children abut their experience growing up in India or, if they have young children, how their daily life is shaped today. I have been surprised to learn that many parents rarely talk about their life stories with their children. Children enjoy listening to these stories as long as you do not go into too many details and make the stories interesting and age-appropriate. One note, usually once the child is nine or ten years old, he is likely to lose interest in your stories.

**When grandparents pay a visit**

If your parents visit, have them talk about their childhoods and how it is different than their grandchildren's. Of course, this will only work if your children are young enough to listen to these stories and old enough to understand: somewhere between the age of five to eleven or so. But if this opportunity comes up, take full advantage of this inter-generation, inter-continental connection.

If possible, take the grandparents to school to talk about their childhood experiences — especially if your children are of elementary school age.

# ❦ 8 ❦

# Communication: Your Key to Family Bliss!

If there is only one key to happiness within a family, it is the key of communication. So many emotional heartaches can be avoided if family members can communicate with each other in a manner that is civilized and open and respectful to every member of the family. In fact, the art of communication is essential in achieving success in life — no matter what career one chooses, if children learn good communication skills at home, they will already be at an advantage when they venture out in the world.

Unfortunately, communication is also the hardest thing to do within a family. Partly because of all the emotional undercurrents and partly because of our close encounters with each other. We are all products of our circumstances. Husband and wife almost always have different ideas when it comes to parenting. How much discipline, how to discipline, what is acceptable and what is not, what to emphasize in a young life — there are so many issues and when they come together to try to raise a child, all of these issues meet head-on. There can be power struggles, emotional outbursts, and financial issues to deal with. No wonder communication is so hard.

According to Suzette Haden Elgin, the author of *The Gentle Art of Communicating with kids*, good communication skills are crucial since it is tightly linked with success. On the flip side, she notes that verbal violence and physical violence are also tightly linked.

119

She writes that, "It is nice to be able to give your children training in tennis, and golf, and ballet, and piano. These skills can be a help in adult life but nothing will help kids as much, and go as far toward making them successful and independent adults, as good language skills."

When you are able to communicate with your children better, you reap multiple benefits. First of all, you remain more informed about what is going on in your child's life, your family life is harmonious and your kids feel comfortable coming to you for anything. You are also able to share family stories. But most of all you will be able to influence their lives in many significant ways since they would not "tune you out" when you are saying something.

Good communication is based on parents demonstrating the following:

▷ sensitivity,

▷ patience (allowing time for communication),

▷ respecting the child's feelings

▷ acknowledging the child's fears and fantasys,

▷ keeping a sense of humor

▷ sharing your own weaknesses, strengths, and concerns,

▷ creating a safe environment, free of criticism,

▷ knowing when to give advice,

▷ knowing when not to say anything,

▷ maintaining the tone of your voice,

▷ taking a real interest in what they enjoy (music, friends, etc.),

▷ restraining from using guilt to motivate.

# Want to communicate with your children better?

The skill to communicate effectively should be rated high — very high — on the list of learning skills as we grow up. Although being a good communicator is an effective tool anywhere, communication becomes extremely vital as we become parents. In fact, communication is crucial to any healthy parent-child relationship. Of course, there are several reasons why communicating with children is important but one main reason is that through communication (verbal and non-verbal), we pass on our values, our emotions, our ideas, our fears, and our vision for the future generation. The following are some basic guidelines for parents to help them fine-tune their communications skills.

**Learn to Listen**

Most people associate communicating with expressing their own views, and forget that listening actively is equally, if not more, important in any effective communication. This is especially true for parents since children often need only a listening ear. Actually if your child knows that you have fully listened and understood what she had to say, she will often surprise you with her own solution. Children are not looking for you to help; they are looking for you to listen!

**Use words in the right measure**

It is not only what you say but also how much you say and when you speak that matters in any communication. We, as parents, often get into a "lecture" mode and say too much. This dilutes what you have to say since now you have added much more to the point you wanted to make. Children are smarter than we give them credit for. They "get" it much sooner than we think, so just making a point is good enough.

### Remember that timing matters

What can be very funny and informative at dinnertime can have a "nuisance" value when your child is rushing out the door. What can be a great topic in a long car ride may be boring at nighttime. Recognize when it is the right time to share and when it is the right time to be brief. This small yet important rule will bring you more results than you imagine.

### Watch for your tone and style

Have you noticed that the same idea when said in an authoritative tone may turn you off but said in a friendly tone perks up your interest? Even children, without knowing, respond to your tone of voice by either offering you an attentive mind or tuning out from what you are saying.

### Be non-judgmental

For instance, when your child offers information about his friend, be open. Take this opportunity to show how you do not judge any person from his actions alone. Children sense your prejudices and opinions right away and then stop sharing their views with you, shrugging "What's the use?"

**Take an interest**

Often parents, who are already stressed with their own activities, find small talks with young children uninteresting. If your child is sharing small details about what happened in the classroom today or what happened in the school bus today, take interest. This is especially true for very young children since they are most likely to share such small details and they are often not very articulate in expressing the event. They can try your patience but remember that the time spent now will help you build a lasting relationship for life.

**Speak softly in order to be heard**

We often believe that by raising our voice, we make a clear statement that should not be taken lightly. Quite the contrary is true. When you raise your voice, your children may hear you loud and clear but do not receive what you are saying. Instead try lowering your voice and notice the impact.

# 9

# *Traditions: Creating a Connection to Your Roots*

A single drop of water, falling constantly, has the power to hollow a stone!

## The hidden value of traditions

A couple of years ago, as we were visiting one older relative, we found out that both of them, along with their son, daughter-in-law and new-born grandson were making a family trip to India. Knowing how difficult it is for the younger couple to take time off from work, not to mention the difficulties and the amount of money involved in making this trip, I asked them what was the purpose of their trip. The answer intrigued me. It was the family tradition to visit a particular small temple in their native town in India whenever there is an addition in the family and since the grandson was the most recent addition in their family, they wanted to make this entire trip. Although the time and re-sources involved in making such a trip may sound unreasonable, I was impressed by the way a tradition can tie the entire family to a small town which otherwise would never be visited by the young couple in the busy lives they lead here.

It took me a long time (I guess it is called growing up) to appreciate the value of traditions. As a teenager, I remember looking down on traditions and people who blindly followed them, since in my mind they represented something from an old era without any flexibility or creativity. I know I am not alone. Often traditions conjure up an image of something from the "Old World." This is because we often associate traditions with outdated ways of doing things that do not make any sense in the lives that we live today. It is also because traditions may come across as rigid and inflexible observations. There is some truth to that. Traditions can be a leftover lifestyle and may be outdated. But they also offer a cultural connection to a rich heritage. Especially when you are trying to raise children away from the living culture, so before you throw away your rich heritage of traditions think once again.

Of course, traditions can become a big drain on your energy and time if you try to observe them all and without any flexibility. Here are a few guidelines to keeping traditions and enjoying them too.

**See the cultural connection**

Traditions can be a beautiful way to connect with our heritage, our ancestors, and our family. Every tradition comes into being for a special reason. The beauty of traditions is their diversity: they can be unique to your family or universal for the entire world and everything in between. So understand traditions for what they really are and identify your cultural connection with them first.

**Pick and choose**

If you seem to have inherited many traditions, try to pick out the ones that you can practically keep. One of the drawbacks of a rich cultural heritage is that over a period of time many traditions slip in and, if they remain unexamined, they seem to accumulate just as material possessions accumulate in a home over time. If this is your problem, then take a hard look at what you can and cannot do and pick the ones that are meaningful to you.

**Understand them**

Often we do not feel like observing or celebrating something when our heart is not in it. If you can ask someone in your family why you do a certain thing or how it came to become a tradition, it will help you to feel inspired to practice them in your family. When you know about the significance, you can also help children see the "connection." Traditions are in one sense, a compilation of family stories, understanding the significance of these traditions will encourage you to maintain them.

**Use creativity**

Once you know the real reason behind a tradition, be creative and put a modern spin on the tradition so that you and your family can enjoy it more.

**See the benefit**

Some traditions can help you give that extra-push to "make that trip" or "take a day off." For example, if your family tradition has been to take a first-born to a specific temple in your hometown in India, see if you can make that long-awaited family trip to India. When you see this trip as a way to connect to your roots, while having a family vacation, it may sound more appealing.

**Be flexible**

One of the biggest problems of any hand-me-down tradition is that they can be rigid and burdensome. But there is always room for some flexibility. For example, if the first haircut of a child is associated with a certain tradition, see if you can meet the "required" tradition by sending the lock of the first haircut. This may sound silly at first, but by at least keeping the tradition within the family, you may gain a longer-term benefit that may otherwise be lost by completely throwing it out the door.

### The special value of traditions to Indians outside of India

Traditions offer a special value to Indians living outside of India, since they offer a stronger reason to ask more questions, an opportunity to talk with your children about your family traditions, and can help you establish your roots. They can become a very strong pull to the culture that otherwise may not be so significant in the lives of your family's future generations.

### Create your own

Modern life offers many opportunities to create our own traditions. For example, the Thanksgiving holiday (in America) can be a time for your family to come together every year for some activity such as a Pooja, or playing a certain game. Is there a special way you would like to celebrate graduations in your family? How about sixteenth birthdays? Think of all the opportunities that your current life offers and see if you can add to your family traditions.

# 10

# *Issues that Come Up*

While raising Indian children in America, there are many issues come up that would have been either non-issues in India or would be at least not so powerful. (Of course, there may be other issues in India that may be more powerful there for parents to tackle.) I have tried to talk about many of these issues as they came up in our lives and the lives of many other Indian parents that we talked to. I realize that depending upon your own background, your home environment, and the level of communication in your family, these issues may not relate to everyone in the same way. But as parents it may help you to at least be aware of these issues and how you feel about them. Fortunately, these are the same issues that offer ample opportunities to inject cultural teachings, your ideas, and your fears. So please take the ones that address your concerns and see how you can add your own "ways of thinking" to tackle these issues as they come up in your own family.

# Giving an allowance

Once I heard a father — whose family had recently arrived to America — very proudly talk about how he had "discovered" that allowance can be successfully used as an incentive to teach his children to strive for better grades. I hope he realized the hidden message he was giving to his child when he used an allowance to "buy" better grades.

While shopping with her eight-year-old son, a mother noticed that his desire to buy something — a toy or a gadget – went down as soon as the mother said yes you could buy it, as long as you are using your allowance money.

Should you give an allowance to your children or not? If yes, what is a good age to start giving an allowance? If no, then how do you handle small expenses that he or she may want to incur? These are some of the many questions that surround the issues of allowance giving. Although giving an allowance to children is not an American concept alone, the issue is definitely being discussed in Indian households in America and India today. However, for Indian parents in America, it offers a unique perspective to inject cultural values while de-emphasizing some others. Before you tie an allowance (a monetary reward) with anything of value that should come from within (such a desire to do better in studies), think twice. You might be losing something more valuable than you realize. Similarly, I have seen parents tie an allowance with some household chores. Beware that by doing such things, you may be introducing the concept of getting paid for something that should be his or her duty.

Does that mean you should not give an allowance to your children at all? No, that is not the implication. What I want to point out here is to be careful. Think about it from various angles and what kind of long-term value you are creating in your family. Like everything that you do with your children, this can be one more opportunity for you to interject the cultural component in your child's life. Here are some of the points to think about.

Should you give your child allowance? What are your reasons for giving it? Is that because you want to teach financial responsibility? Is it because you think it is the "right" thing to do? Whatever may be your reasons, go over them and make a conscious decision about starting an allowance.

Anything that we do with our children gives us an opportunity to impart some value to them. Giving an allowance to children is similarly an excellent opportunity for us to introduce them to some hidden values. Here are some suggestions:

### Emphasize the value of "rights" vs. "duties"

It is very common in most families to couple the child's right to an allowance with doing chores. As much as this sounds like a right thing to do, think of it slightly differently. Do you offer an allowance as a "pay" for some jobs done or do you offer an allowance because the child is also a part of the family? Here is an excellent opportunity to tell your child that as a family member it is his right to receive an allowance as soon as he is old enough to need one. Just like any other need a child has that has been fulfilled by a family, this is also a need and is being taken care of by his family. However, (and here is the key) as a member of the family, it is his duty to help out. So the allowance is not "tied" to a specific task but it is his right just as helping out is his duty.

### Emphasize the value of giving

Allowance is also an excellent way to teach the value of giving. Is there any cause that is close to his heart that he would like to help? Encourage a child to figure out a way to help someone no matter how small the contribution.

### Emphasize the value of saving

Talk to your children about the value of saving some portion of their "income." Open an account in her name. Take her to the bank, show her the chart of growth, and talk about the effect of compounding if your child is old enough to understand.

### Emphasize the value of contentment

It can take the skill of a negotiator to decide how much is enough when it comes to giving an allowance. By talking about how to derive a sense of contentment and how "there is never enough in life for the people who are never content" you can emphasize the value of gratitude for what we have. Of course all of us know that it is not easy to teach this to children, but at least it provides one more opportunity to do so.

### Teach the history of money

This may be a good time talk about the history of money, the barter system and how people handled money in earlier times. There are many good books out there that children can read and understand.

We often do not realize it, but no matter what your child grows up to be, a doctor, a painter, or a lawyer, he or she will have to learn how to handle money. Almost everything that a person knows about money comes solely from their upbringing. So handling an allowance can be a good start in that learning process.

# Establishing curfew time

If there is one issue that can cause more trouble than it is worth, it is the issue of a curfew, the time that a child is expected home at night. Much friction stems from negotiating this time, which is similar to the issues surrounding bedtime. As your children grow slightly older, you stretch bedtime slightly further. Similarly, start the curfew time at some reasonable time, and then as you find your teenager behaving more responsibly, you will be able to increase the time that he or she can be away from home.

One major bone of contention that seems to come up in most families is that they may have different curfew times for boys and girls. This can spell trouble! Make sure that you have the same curfew time for your children and that whatever difference there may be, it is related to age and not gender.

Also setting up this time in advance can relieve a lot of the stress of negotiating when the child is ready to walk out the door. Try not to make any exceptions.

Just like bedtime, be reasonable in deciding the time, but once you have established a curfew time, enforce it clearly and equally. Do not decide on an event-by-event basis because this is a sure way to create friction in the future.

One way to reward your teenagers is by allowing them a later curfew time if you find them to be respecting the overall rules of staying out.

# Household chores

Often household chores are one place where two cultures clash head on. That is because U.S. and Indian cultures look at household chores differently, and this perspective may tie-in with the way the family unit is regarded by each culture.

Teaching and expecting children to help out from the time they are young helps them feel like more confident and caring members of the family. Here is what I found helpful:

**Start early**

Even very young children are capable of helping their moms and dads. Get them involved as early as three or four years of age.

**Make it fun**

Many, almost all, household tasks can be fun if you make it playful enough.

**Keep some flexibility**

Although "assigning" a task makes a child more responsible toward it, it can also become drudgery. Build some flexibility into your assignments. Flexibility and fun make work seem enjoyable.

**Keep tasks simple and age appropriate**

Knowing clearly what is expected of you makes it much easier to accomplish the task and feel fulfilled. Instead of being vague –"help out in the kitchen after dinner" — say "clear the table" after dinner.

**Rotate**

We all get tired of doing the same thing over and over. Come up with a creative way to rotate the work. For example, at the beginning of every week let everyone pick a note from a basket and discover their assignment for the week.

**Know what you want to teach**

Helping out teaches children much. It boosts their confidence; it makes them feel part of the family; it offers interaction; it can start a dialogue regarding why things are done in a certain way; it can nudge their creativity (I remember reading about one child who "invented" a special handle for milk containers since they were too heavy for him to lift, and he realized that it may be a problem for some elderly people as well). Be mindful of these side benefits, and use them to emphasize the value that you want to teach.

**Be aware of cultural differences**

In India, doing chores for family and neighbors is a part of growing up and comes naturally to most people. Of course, this is different across economic and social lines but by and large it is generally true. In western culture almost everyone is expected to help in household chores. The main difference is that in India it is unthinkable to offer money to a child — even a neighbor's child — for running an errand or helping out. Whereas in America, a child may get paid when he or she helps even his own parents. (Please see "Giving Allowance" for the pros and cons of monetary rewards).

**Make it a family time**

Some tasks such as setting the table or helping clean the kitchen after dinner can also become a family time. Since everyone is around working, it can become a nice time to share the day's events.

# Taking your children to a pooja

*Havan, pooja, bhajan,*and other religious activities are the life-sustaining activities of a Hindu community, and since almost every important event in a person's life is an occasion to perform a *pooja* or a *Havan* where including extended family members and friends is normal, children participate in these events. These activities offer a wonderful opportunity to teach our children the fundamentals of pooja rituals, some slokas, and some religious stories. In fact, these events are so beautifully intertwined that it is amazing to see how religion and social needs are seamlessly integrated within a society. For example, a *Satyanarayan pooja* can combine ritualistic aspects, storytelling, and delicious food all in one event.

Exposing young children to these events can be a great help in teaching aspects of Hindu culture. It can also help start communication about many aspects of religion, the reasons behind traditions, the age of a particular story from which the pooja is rendered, etc. Despite these benefits it is often difficult for parents of young children to coax them to go to such events. Here are some ways to make this easier:

### Know their attention span

If you want your children to appreciate and understand pooja, or any other religious ceremony, learn to respect their attention span. Often a long-winded pooja can be the most boring time for a young mind. If you have to stay at a pooja where you think it is going to test your children's patience, offer them other alternatives. While it is great to teach your children discipline and proper behavior during religious events, know how much to try and when to let go.

### Get them involved

Children love doing things. Can you find ways to keep them engaged in a religious ceremony? There are small ways you can get them involved.

**Keep the time short for very young children**

For very young children, under three, there is not much you can do to keep them occupied beyond a certain time. Let them soak in the environment for half an hour to an hour and then take them in other room or give them something else to do.

**Explain to them what is going on**

If possible, ask the priest to explain in English so that children can understand. There are many priests today who know how to make it kid-friendly.

**Do not expect too much**

Spirituality and religion are very subtle imprints and it will take a long time before they will bear fruits of their own. In the meantime, just offer an environment where these ceremonies can be soaked in.

# Teaching fundamental aspects of performing a pooja

Religious ceremonies, and rituals are the backbone of Hindu life and almost every important event in one's life is marked by some ceremony that includes invoking the family deity, performing pooja, and making offerings to bless the event. Teaching the fundamental discipline about how to perform pooja may include lighting a lamp or performing an aarti, will help children participate in the ceremony.

Some of the key things to teach are:

▷ How to light a lamp (for slightly older children).

▷ How to accept prasaad, the blessed food that is offered usually at the end of any ceremony.

▷ How to perform the aarti.

▷ How to do the tilak on someone or themselves.

▷ How to do the rosary (mala).

Since every family is unique in these aspects, it is difficult to make a list of all the items that are part of performing a pooja, but think of some of the simple rituals and try to teach them at age appropriate times. Like teaching anything else, it is important to point out that your kids will be eager to learn this earlier rather than later so start when they are young before they develop negative attitudes. Get them involved in doing part of a pooja at regular intervals; every morning, once a week, or once a month. Make that a part of your routine while they are young. Here are some of the things you can do to teach fundamental aspects of a Pooja:

▷ Familiarize your child with Pooja items such as divi (lamp holder), bell, aarti, Kumkum, etc.

▷ Involve them in small gestures like chiming bells, distributing prasaad.

▷ Introduce them to different gods and goddesses pictures and statues.

▷ Teach some simple slokas.

▷ Keep it simple.

▷ Introduce them to mala (rosary beads).

▷ Teach them simple breathing exercise.

## Teaching an Indian language

Experts know that childhood is the best time to learn any language. Not only is a child capable of learning multiple languages concurrently but he is also able to master these languages better if introduced during the first five years of age. Authors Edith Harding and Philip Riley, of *The Bilingual Family: A Handbook for Parents* advise that "Broadly speaking, very small children seem to learn two languages simultaneously as they would learn one: they have bilingualism as a mother tongue. Children below about eight years of age are most unlikely to need any formal teaching or language lessons. The best way to encourage the acquisition of a new language for the child is to have happy experiences with friendly persons in sympathetic surroundings, where learning is spontaneous and done quite unconsciously."

However, a problem may occur when the parents spend less time with the child. Often it is not which one but how to teach the language that is the issue. If you speak that language then it will not be difficult for the child to learn it, at least the speaking aspect of the language. There are so many language schools now throughout the country that finding one near you may not be that big a problem. So no matter how your child learns one of the Indian languages, there are a few tips for you to remember.

Make your child feel comfortable talking in that language. Often adults find it funny the way the child speaks in their language, and kids sense that and feel uncomfortable. Make sure that no one laughs when your child is using another language.

As much as possible, soak your child in the environment of that language. This will mean music, maybe some videotape of the stories in that language, and of course speaking around him.

If you and your partner speak two different languages, do not be afraid to expose her to both the languages. It will only enrich her total experience.

As your child grows, provide him with enhanced levels of the language. For example, try to get books for different age levels in your language.

# Sleepovers

While talking with parents, I was surprised to find that sleepovers are one of the most debated issues between husbands and wives. In many parents' minds sleepovers, just as dating, come with a loaded meaning. Of course as parents, we worry about the safety of our children and somehow knowing that they are safe in their own beds at nighttime makes it easy for us to sleep better. It is also worrisome, for many parents, to send a child to someone's house for the night. This seems to matter the most for girls. Maybe because in India, many families believe that young girls should not stay out at night and should spend the night at home. This belief of course has its roots is keeping daughters safe from unforeseen dangers that lurk at nighttime. Whatever the reasons, sleepovers have been a matter of arguments in many households around the country. So here are some things that can help you deal with the issue.

▷ Get to know the family. Knowing the family will put a lot of your concerns at ease.

▷ Ration the number of sleepovers if you feel that your child is not ready for too many overnights.

▷ Invite their friends to your home.

▷ Offer to pick them up late at night. So-called "pajama parties" are becoming quite popular with very young kids. Parents pick the little sleepy and tired ones up at midnight.

▷ Find out what activities are planned.

▷ Talk to the parents and share your concerns, if you think it is appropriate.

▷ Make sure both you and your spouse feel comfortable with the arrangements.

A note: The appropriate age to begin sleepovers, according to some experts, is six or seven depending upon the child, of course. It helps the child in his sense of independence and how to behave in other people's homes.

## Peer pressure

Much has been written about peer pressure in almost all the media since it is a major area of concern for most parents, Indian or not. However, peer pressure may be slightly overrated in terms of concerns since if the upbringing is healthy during the first ten years of a child's life and if the communication within the family is good, peer pressure will become less of an issue in teenage years. Having said that, in the tentative years of adolescence, peer pressure can be a real threat. How do you as parents counter it? Here are some pointers to help you:

**Trust your teachings**

Luckily, a baby is born without any attitude or pre-conceived notions! You are given a few years (usually about seven or nine, depending upon the child), to create a bond, an environment and an atmosphere of communication. If you have done the job right during the early years, you may have less to worry during adolescent years. Your initial samskars will eventually win over peer pressure – at least to some degree. Often we do not put enough trust in our teachings and our children.

**Keep communication open**

These are the years when having better communication with your children will help. Make your child feel comfortable sharing his problems. They are also going through difficult times and if they feel confident that they can share some of their concerns with you, they will be less likely to fall prey to peer pressure.

**Acknowledge the problem**

Peer pressure is a real problem for most of us at some time or another. Talk about how you dealt with it in your childhood, how many of your friends dealt with it, and if you have experiences related to this topic, share them. This acknowledgement will reassure your children.

**Know their friends**

As much as possible, stay involved in their lives. At the dinner table, talk about who their friends are, what they do, etc. The more you know their peers, the less you will feel threatened.

**Refrain from passing judgments**

Often we make the mistake of making sweeping remarks about a certain way of doing things, a different hairstyle, a habit of a person from a different background or different views. These comments send signals to children that we already have an opinion about their friends. When our children feel that we are open to different ideas, they will feel less threatened.

**Watch your own life**

A teenage daughter of a friend of mine pointed out once that her mom tells her that what her friends think is not important, while her mother is always working hard to please her own friends. Parents are not immune to peer pressure and if we do not set a good example, our children will have a harder time with it.

# Vegetarian or not

Lately in America, being a vegetarian is becoming very common. Many young boys and girls choose to be vegetarian. Depending upon your own background and religious beliefs, this issue can become important or not. Being vegetarian is neither just an Indian thing nor is it observed throughout India. But since culturally non-violence is one of the highly regarded values in Indian culture, many parts of India and especially the Jain community are very strict about being vegetarian.

Hindus believe that the food you eat is directly associated with the kind of thoughts you may have and because of that eating vegetarian food is considered to be a better aid in the spiritual journey.

There are several health reasons to be a vegetarian as well. Since the majority of the population in India has vegetarian, the cooking is evolved around a lot of vegetables and spices. So if your child decides to become a vegetarian, he or she may want to learn the variety of Indian cooking.

Obviously there are no right and wrong answers but there are facts that you can point out. Luckily for children growing up today, being vegetarian is not unusual as the movement toward being vegetarian is gaining momentum. It is also easy to find food while eating outside the home if you are a vegetarian. There are many restaurants that cater to this group. Of course, there are health benefits for people who are vegetarian as well. If your child chooses to be a vegetarian, then the previous explanation will help him explain to his friends why he believes it is wrong to eat meat.

If your child is a vegetarian, then you may want to make sure that he or she knows how to cook many of the vegetarian dishes. Today there are many good books available so that may not be very difficult.

One of the things you can do if your children choose to be vegetarian is to teach them how to answer some of the questions that are being asked by others who are not familiar with a vegetarian lifestyle. Questions such as where he or she gets her protein to why is he or she a vegetarian.

# Instilling spirituality

> "One of the best things that happened to our children while they
> were growing up [was the] visits of several spiritual leaders to our
> home. Our children were able to ask questions and understand
> some of the finer aspects of spirituality directly from these leaders
> and [these interactions] made them understand complex issues."
> —comment by parents of now grown and successful children.

It has been said, "You are not a human being having a spiritual
experience but you are a spiritual being having a human experience." Spirituality has been a very significant part of Indian
cultural life and a guiding force in every aspect. Religion and
spirituality have been the source of strength and direction for
the entire society. As an Indian parent, you will either directly
or indirectly instill the value of spirituality in your children. In
fact, Indian culture is so interwoven with spirituality that it is
hard to separate the two.

Spirituality offers your children a way to feel connected to something greater than themselves and to have an internal support
system that they can always call on. It also helps them ride out
the ups and downs that life brings with a sense of understanding
and detachment. Of course most of the aspects of religion and
spirituality will be learned from you, at least in the initial years
of their lives. Later you can provide other sources to quench
their thirst for knowledge.

If you are interested in specifically giving the value of spirituality there are many books and websites that offer you ways
to introduce your children to Hindu scriptures, thoughts, and

analysis. One such website with a wealth of information is http://www.avgsatsang.org offered by Arsh Vidya Gurukulam in Pennsylvania. Himalayan Academy also has a very nice collection of information, books and news: www.himalayanacademy.com

It is also vital to have some religious books such as *Gita Ramayana* and *Mahabharata* in your home. Exposure to these books from early childhood will help in fostering spirituality in your children.

When your children get slightly older, may be about eight or nine, have discussions about spirituality, God, truth, etc. It will help your child to think about these issues and will create a sense of curiosity that can become the starting point for a life-long search for answers.

If possible, introduce them to spiritual leaders by visiting an Ashram. Such visits will introduce them to a lifestyle that is different than what they may get to see around them regularly.

## Talking about misconceptions

Many a times a child may feel uncomfortable about her background because she does not understand or is not able to explain, some of the complex aspects of her culture and religion. Again, in an environment where everyone shares similar values, she may not be ridiculed or questioned about these issues, but in a foreign environment other kids will have questions or will point out things that they find very odd.

One of the best ways to handle this is to equip your children with basic information and prepare them to answer some of the most common questions. Even if they are not put into a situation where they are called upon to explain some of the misconceptions, it might be a good idea to talk to them about these issues at an age-appropriate time.

**Many gods**

One of the most noted and discussed aspect of Hinduism is that it has many gods. Children who are born into other religions find it difficult to understand this and often question Indian children. It can be baffling for young ones to explain such a complex issue. Here is an explanation in nutshell: The truth is that Hindus all worship One Supreme God. However it is called by different names depending upon the background and language that one speaks. Something like a situation where the same individual may be known by different names and may be identified as uncle or brother or boss.

**Belief in reincarnation**

Hindus believe that the soul is immortal and takes birth time and time again. This is so that it will finally evolve spiritually and be freed from taking physical birth. This is a hard concept for children to understand and they may have many questions. Their friends may also ask them questions about reincarnation. Depending upon the age of your children explain to them that we believe that God gives us many chances to grow by giving us a new birth.

**The theory of Karma**

The theory of Karma according to the Hindu philosophy is the universal principle of cause and effect. It simply tells us that every action will bring fruits and through our actions we decide our future, and this then helps us in becoming better people by encouraging us to do good actions. Karma is an often-misunderstood word that can be erroneously interpreted by Westerners as destiny.

## Cow worship

Hindus believe that a cow symbolizes the all-giving, sustaining earth. She is a symbol of grace and gentleness, and because she provides us with milk, she is equivalent to our mother. Although it looks like Hindus worship the cow, actually Hindus show reverence to all living beings, including plants and vegetables.

## Dot on the forehead

Dot or a bindi (tilak) in the middle of a forehead is a distinctive mark of Hinduism and it signifies the third eye. Women also use this dot as a beauty mark and as a part of make-up. Since it is different than Western make-up kids often ask their parents the reason behind this mark, and the simple explanation can be that it is a beauty mark.

## The caste system

India, being the oldest living culture, has evolved a social system that was once based upon a person's occupation. This is similar to European society with its artisans' guilds and other organizations. However, in India, these caste systems became a stronger bond during thousands of years of foreign rule (when people felt more secured dealing with their own kind) and the caste system was strengthened. Although intact in many parts of India, the caste system is losing its grip in larger cities and in other pockets of India.

# 11

# *Samskara Ceremonies*

In Hindu culture, Samskara ceremonies play a very significant role. They offer a higher sanctity, and just as any precious stone needs refining and polishing, samskara ceremonies are supposed to purify and polish the individual so that he can shine at his best. The earliest traces of Samskara ceremonies are found in Rig Veda. They are essentially key points in a person's life when different gods and goddesses have been invoked and worshipped to seek blessings for the growth of a person. Since most of the "firsts" happen at the time when a child is very young (such as name-giving, first eating of solid food, etc.) most samskara ceremonies are performed for a young child. Although there are many samskara ceremonies, there are sixteen most significant samskara in one's life. Here is the list of those sixteen samskara in the order in which they are performed.

1. Impregnation (*Garbhadhan* Samskara)

2. Fetus Protection (*Punsavan* Samskara)

3. Satisfying the cravings of a pregnant mother (*Simantonayan* Samskara)

4. Childbirth (*Jaat karma* Samskara)

5. Giving the child a name (*Namkaran* Samskara)

6. First outing of the child from home (*Nishkraman* Samskara)

7.  Giving the child solid food (*Annaprashan* Samskara)

8.  Shaving the child's head (*Chaulkarma* Samskara)

9.  Piercing the child's ears (*Karnavedha* Samskara)

10. *Yagnopavit*Samskara (*Upnayan* Samskara)

11. Starting the study of Vedas (*Vedarambh* Samskara)

12. Returning home after completing education (*Samavartan* Samskara)

13. Marriage (*Vivah* Samskara)

14. Invoking ancestors (*Sanyasta* Samskara)

15. *Vanaprastha*

16. Cremation (*Antim* Samskara)

All of the above samskara were held in significance in ancient times since they were interconnected with the lifestyle, there is a few that still hold power to influence a growing child. I have tried to discuss them here: what they are, how to perform the ceremony, and the significance of the ceremonies.

**Impregnation (Garbhadhan Samskara)**

This Samskara ceremony is essentially one to offer prayers to deities to help a bride conceive happy and healthy children. The prayers involve saying something to the effect that "may we produce strong and long-lived children, may they be well behaved, bright and wealthy. May God make us fit for conception."

Since procreation is considered a pious duty of everyone unless someone is physically unfit, impregnation ceremonies are the beginning of a child's life.

**Punsavanam**

This Samskara are given during the third or fourth month of pregnancy. On a special day a few drops of juice from the banyan stem are put on the right nostril of the mom-to-be. According to Sushruta – the great Ayurveda writer –the juice of a banyan tree has all the properties to relieve any trouble during pregnancy. A sacred thread is tied to her left wrist while the prayer mantras are chanted.

The father of the child puts his hand on the stomach of his pregnant wife and chants a mantra from Yajur Veda which loosely means: "O Soul in the womb, May you have the swiftness of a nice-winged swift bird, may there arise in your head the combination of action, contemplation, and learning. May Gayatri be your eyes, Brihat and Rathantara like your sides, Rig-Veda your soul, metres your limbs. May you acquire knowledge and attain happiness in this life and beyond."

**Simantonayan Samskara**

This is one of the important Samskara ceremonies and is usually performed during the fifth and eighth months of pregnancy. The goal is to invoke the deity and pray for a trouble-free delivery and the birth of a sharp and intelligent child. This Samskara is performed in the presence of family members and friends. Many parents in America perform this ceremony along with a "baby shower."

During this ceremony, family deities, Ganesha, and other Gods are invoked, epics are narrated and mantras are chanted because it is believed that learning begins when the baby is in mother's womb and if you want your child to remember something for the rest of his or her life, this is the time to sing it to him or her. It is also believed that this ceremony will ensure trouble free delivery and a birth of a healthy child.

## Name-giving (Namakaran) ceremony

For Hindus, Namakaran samskara is one of the sixteen most significant samskars in a person's life. The ceremony essentially welcomes the baby while all the relatives can offer their blessings to the newborn. Any elderly relative or priest can perform the ceremony.

Select a day — preferably the 12$^{th}$ day after the birth, but any day thereafter, to perform the ceremony.

Give the baby a bath and put new clothes on the baby. You will need *Kumkum*, *Haldi*, a fresh flower garland, anklets and bracelets for the baby, a coconut, ghee, honey, and sweets.

The priest or an elderly person says, "We are gathered here to offer a name to the child of [say the names of both the parents]."

The ceremony starts with the veneration to Shri Ganesha.

There are a few slokas the priest will recite. Here is the meaning of those slokas in a nutshell.

"We seek blessings of Gods and elders for this child and request them to make this day auspicious for the sacrament."

"Oh God, we should hear and see only that which helps us to be better persons. We will lead the life given by you with health and vigor."

"We are performing the sacrament of naming this child. Please bless it."

"Now we will felicitate the mother who has given birth to this child. Mother carries the child in her womb for nine months. She feeds it, nourishes it, looks after it and brings it up. Its body, mind, and soul are built up by her alone. So worship your mother. May her mother-in-law offer her coconut (indicating desired progeny). May her father-in-law give her new clothes. Let her husband offer her a flower garland. Other relations may offer her congratulations and offer their blessings and gifts."

(Feed the child a mixture of ghee and honey, the symbol of life energy, to bring radiant health, a sound mind, and a sharp intellect.)

"Now we will offer him the name. Say, "Your name is. . . ." Three times.

"May your name reach the remote corners of the world with fame."

(Offer new clothes, anklets, and a bracelet to the baby.)

For a newborn son:

"May you have a long life. May you be a hero and a savior like Bhagvan Krishna and Bhagvan *Rama*. May you be a noble soul like *Shankaracharya*, *Ramdas*, and *Vivekananda*. May you be a leader like *Vikramaditya* or *Shivaji*. May you attain wealth, name, and fame."

For a newborn daughter:

"May you have a long life. May you be a learned woman like *Gargi* and *Maitraiyi*. May you have a character like *Sita* and *Savitri*. May you be a devotee like *Meera* and *Mukta*. May you be brave like Queen of *Zansi*. May you attain wealth, name, and fame."

**Yagnopavit Samskara**

Also known as the Sacred Thread Ceremony or Upnayan samskara, Yagnopavit samskara is ideally performed at the age of eight years of age and signals the onset of Brahmacharya ashram, a time in life when the pursuit of knowledge is of prime importance. In Vedic times, the student used to leave his house to stay with his "guru." Of course in modern times the child stays with his parents.

According to the script, the pursuit of "Brahman" (the truth), is Brahmacharya and there are six specific steps to achieve or speed up the process. They involve taking food that enriches the mind, exercise that gives strength, activities that control the senses, prayers, self-study, and study with the guru and character building.

Also in contrast to the prevalent belief, in Vedic times both boys and girls were initiated in the pursuit of knowledge and given the Yagnopavit samskara. It is only in the later times, when girls found themselves restrained in their freedom (due to foreign invasions) that only boys started getting the samskara since it was associated with leaving home and girls did not leave home.

The essence of this sacrament is to take the vow of studenthood; students from any caste, creed, or even religion can undergo this samskara. Traditionally, one month prior to the sacrament, students should be explained the meaning and significance of this samskara. Following are the brief steps to explain the ceremony:

1. The vow of Brahmacharyaashram: During this part of the ceremony, the aspiring student asks this question to the priest and the priest explains the meaning.

2. The value of knowledge: In this part of the ceremony the priest explains the value of knowledge to the aspiring student.

3. Code of conduct of the Brahmacharyaashram: Now the priest explains the required code of conduct in order to pursue knowledge. It involves:

   1. balance in diet and activities,

   2. control of organs of senses and action,

   3. daily prayers and meditation, self study and discourses,

   4. service to the guru, and

   5. developing strength in personality and character.

4. Wearing the sacred thread: In this part of the ceremony the priest gives the sacred thread and shows how to wear it and take care of it properly.

5. Giving Gayatri mantra: Now the priest gives the Gayatri mantra to the student and explains the meaning of the mantra briefly.

   Irrespective of your decision to give this samskara to your child, you can try to incorporate the message of the ceremony in his or her upbringing by emphasizing the six codes of conduct that are a vital part of the Samskara.

### Samavartan samskara

This is the samskara typically performed when the child returns home after completing his studies of Veda in the Gurukul. This Samskara indicates the end of Brahmacharayashram (the life of celibacy) so now the graduate had to choose between the Grihashthashrama (the life of a householder) or renunciation. The word Samavartan literally means "returning home from the home of the guru." This samskara may be performed along with the sacred thread (Yagnopavit) samskara as well.

In modern days this Samskara is similar to a graduation ceremony. Indian parents can replace graduation parties with Samavartan Samskara or include that as a part of the graduation party.

If you want you can perform this samskara with Havan Pooja after your child's graduation from university. Here are some of the instructions that were traditionally given to the student who was leaving the guru's ashram after completion of studies.

▷ Always speak the truth.

▷ Practice Dharma

▷ Do not neglect the study of Vedas

▷ Do not neglect prosperity

▷ Do not neglect your duties to the gods

▷ Treat your mother, father, teacher and guest as gods

These instructions are as applicable to today's graduate as it was to a student of Vedas thousands of years ago. In a graduation ceremony, we can include Samavartan Samskara and offer these teachings to the young graduate.

12 

# Creating a Cultural Connection through Music and Dance

When we chose Bharatnatyam for our daughter we had no idea how to go about selecting the kind of dance for her. All we knew was that we had heard very high praise for the teacher in our area. We also did not know much about the other similar dances so our choice was not the most informed one given that she studied this for the next nine years, put in hours of practice, and we spent thousands of dollars. I want to provide young parents today with some basic information to make their decision a more informed one. What we did not know then, and know now, is that learning Bharatnatyam — actually any classical dance form — helps a young girl during her puberty years in building her self-confidence as well as enhances her sense of self.

Art and literature are really the two strong pillars of any culture and learning art –any art– be it dance, music, drama, etc., brings the culture alive. For parents who are raising their children away from their own culture, art can be a great bridge to help their children understand and appreciate their cultural heritage. It also provides a strong connection to other U.S. born Indian children, as well as to children in India. Especially when these children grow up and go into Universities, they find themselves sharing their talent and culture with others with pride.

There are so many things to choose from. Even if you decide that dance is the right art to pursue, you will have to choose what form of dance. The same goes for music or art. Each of these art forms has classical roots but there are the folk versions. Decide if you want the folk art or the classical form.

Of course, I have to admit that I am biased toward the classical form of any of these arts although I am aware of the benefits folk dances and music bring to people's lives. I feel that since a lot of resources of time and money are spent on learning these disciplines, the best use of those resources is when a truly classical form is being mastered or understood.

Here are some points for you to consider before you decide where you want to spend your time and energy:

**Think long term**

Whatever your child learns at this time, will stay for a very long time with him so choose something that he can enjoy for a long time. For example, learning to play a musical instrument will bring pleasure for a very long time as compared to learning folk dances.

**Think classical**

Actually the concerns are the same as above. Anything that is classical will have a long staying power as opposed to anything that is popular. Also, any classical art will provide the child with a sense of identity and discipline, as any classical art requires a tremendous amount of discipline to master.

**Think about your home environment**

Though our daughter was learning both classical music and dance, I felt that she was learning music with much more interest simply because our home environment was more conducive to learning music as opposed to the dance. Consider what is easily available in your household. Take advantage of the environment that already exists in the family.

**Keep in mind the value of art**

Art and literature have a special value that is hard to quantify in terms of money or other achievements. It is really the unfolding of self, a way to connect to God, and a special way to enjoy life. So giving children the gift of art is one of the best gifts a parent can give.

**Think about the kind of teacher you can get in your area**

Although as the Indian community grows in America there are several very good choices of teachers for any of these art forms, you will still need to evaluate the level of teaching your child will receive in any selected art form.

The following are the most commonly learned dance forms from India. I have just briefly described what they are for parents who may not be familiar with them. When you are considering dance for your daughter — or son — consider the pointers that I have mentioned above. Also use this description to see if there is any particular one that will appeal to you better.

# Classical dances

# Bharatnatyam

One of the most popular, and also one of the oldest forms of Indian classical dances in America, Bharatnatyam enjoys a special place in Indian culture already. Based on a balanced distribution of body weight, Bharatnatyam is a beautiful, vibrant and an extremely disciplined art form. It offers discipline of body and mind and it is a complete art form according to Jothi Raghavan, the founder of a Nrityanjali dance school located in Boston for over twenty-five years and a very accomplished dancer herself. Bharatnatyam is a complete art form and as a result, the dancer is able to adapt to other styles quickly and easily. Its training provides them with strong basics in footwork and body movement.

According to *Indian Classical Dance* written by Leela Venkatraman and Avinash Pasricha, the present form of Bharatnatyam was continued defying the ban on court dancing by the British East India Company. The concert format of Alaripu, Jatisswaram, Sabdam, Varnam, Padam, Javeli, and Tillana still follows from early days. In Bharatnatyam, since joints and not muscles dictate movement, the dance tends to be geometrical. There is an elaborate vocabulary of hand gestures used to represent ideas in interpretative dance. Today Bharatnatyam has spread throughout India and now is making its impact on Indians in America and other countries. Since this style of dance has proliferated in Indian social life, there is some mediocrity has also seeped in. So if you want your daughter — or son — to learn Bharatnatyam, try to find the best teacher in your area. Check out her credentials, her commitment, attend her class, and if possible, attend one of her concerts. If you are going to spend so much time, money, and energy, you want to make sure that your child is learning the best that is available to her.

Learning Bharatnatyam is definitely one of the important ways a child growing up outside of India will learn about her culture and the fact that she will have an opportunity to have an "Arangetram" will help her showcase her culture to her peers at the time when she may be trying to understand who she is and what is her identity.

# Kathak

Kathak comes close to Bharatnatyam in popularity amongst Indians living outside of India and it offers a visually beautiful treat. The name Kathak comes from the word "Katha" meaning story, and it is associated with the art of storytellers. This form of dancing began with the idea of storytellers who were part of temples in Northern India. Their story ("katha" from epics) was narrated thru recitation, mime, and gestures. During the 15$^{th}$ and 16$^{th}$ centuries they were brought to the courts of the Muslim kings, and varied slightly in different cities from Jaipur to Lucknow. Their stories also revolved around Radha and Krishna.

Kathak originated and was nurtured primarily in the Uttar Pradesh, Madhya Pradesh, and Rajasthan area of India. It is the only dance style that combines Hindu and Islamic influences. Unlike other forms of Indian classical dances, a Kathak dancer performs erect without the knee bending and without seated poses. The body of the Kathak dancer becomes a percussion instrument where he or she explores the "tala" with the feet. The dancer creates soundscape through footwork and ankle bell sounds. The dancer's upper torso, through a delicate shoulder inclined towards one side, imparts movement and posture with fluid grace.

# Kathakali

Kathakali, most easily identified by the costume and the actor's portraying super-human characters such as gods, demons, and animals, evolved as a combination of artistic influences from Kerala's multiple art forms. The most striking feature of Kathakali dance is the splendor of costumes, facial masks and ornaments.

In order to master the art, the dance requires very high degree of physical discipline with grueling eight to ten hours of daily practice. This dance also requires a the suppleness of the body. Historically Kathakali evolved as an all-male dance, where male artists played the female roles. Make-up plays a large role in Kathakali dances and hand gestures, set to micro rhythms set actors apart. Kathakali is a fine classic dance that requires tremendous energy and discipline. It takes years for a novice to graduate into an actor. Seven years of full-time practice under a meticulous teacher is the minimum requirement. But to make an accomplished actor able to portray versatility, it takes many more years.

# Kuchipudi

Originally from Andhra Pradesh and practiced by all-male Brahmin performers, Kuchipudi is now primarily all-female dance form. It is similar to Bharatnatyam because it is based on Natya Sastra. Historically Kuchipudi would be an all-week affair where the characters of Rukmini, Satyabhama, and Mohini were highly eminent. Although in the past the role of the actor included spoken words as well, today Kuchipudi is only a dance form and whereas the singing is done by the musicians only. It is one of the fast dances within the Indian classical dance art form.

# Manipuri

Manipuri dance comes from the Indo-Mongoloid people as a form of worship symbolizing an intertwined serpent, to evoke divinity. Male and female forms in this dance are distinct and animals feature highly throughout the dance. The ability of male dancers to emulate the gait of an elephant, deer, snake, and swan are part of the training. Manipuri is visually a very different kind of dance than other Indian classical dance forms. Instead of hand movements and intricate footwork, Manipuri is a highly internalized art of expression that requires years of diligent practice. The knees are bent forward instead of sideways as in other dance forms. This dance form is highly ritualistic and draws heavily from legends and mythology. Drums play an important part in this dance. Manipuri is not as common as the other dance forms and finding a teacher may be difficult. Manipuri is still confined to its place of origin, and according to one survey very few people of non-Manipur origin come forward to learn this art form.

## Mohini Attam

This form of dance, which literally means "the dance to enchant," is originally from Kerala, the southern state of India. In the purest form, the dance represents the forces of both sustenance and cohesion. As the story goes, when both gods and demons were churning the ocean in the battle of righteousness, Lord Vishnu took the form of enchantress Mohini to cast a spell of enchantment on the demons and helped the gods to get the pot of elixir. Mohini also helped Lord Shiva in his fight with the demon Bhasmasura who was lured by her beauty. The moves and techniques of Mohini Attam reflect images from Kerala: coconuts swaying in the wind, boats, and water ripples. Mohini is believed to have emerged from the water, so every movement seems to be in a smooth, circular style where the flexibility of waist, shoulders, elbows, and wrists create the dance. Eye movements also play a vital role in the dance. The white costume with a gold border brings dignity and elegance to the dance form.

# Odissi

Originating in the state of Orissa, Odissi, in its modern form began in theaters. Stylistically, Odissi revolves around Tribhanga as the central posture. The head, torso, and lower half of the body are in deflection and each part is bent in opposition to the part above to create a three-bend figure. In its best form the movements look very fluid, but if not rendered properly, they may look jerky. Lately Odissi has gained popularity within India as well as outside of India. Similar to Manipuri, you may find it difficult to find a good teacher of Odissi dance form in your area.

# Classical music

Indian classical music has developed over thousands of years and has roots in spirituality and the science of sound. Fortunately, like many other Indian things, classical music is also gaining in popularity in the West. This makes it easier for parents to encourage their children to learn this beautiful and traditional art of their heritage. Similar to learning any other classical art such as dance, music is not an isolated learning tool but it ties the child to the very roots of Indian culture. He or she learns without realizing the social, cultural, and religious aspects of the culture. Indian classical music is mainly divided in two somewhat diverse systems called Hindustani and Carnatic style, mainly identified as the North Indian and South Indian styles. Here is an introduction to Indian classical music.

# Raga

There are mainly thirty ragas and each one of them has a mood of its own that it helps create. By definition a raga is "that which delights or charms." Raga is nothing but a melodic law or order. A raga consists of at least five notes with some combination of dominant note (vadi) and complementary note (samvadi) and its relation in a raga. The system of Raga is really the backbone of Indian classical or light music. Even the folk music has its basis in Raga. Today's highly codified system of Raga is the result of a very long process of evolution and interaction between folk music and classical music.

# Tala

Tala means "rhythm" and is, of course. not unique to Indian music. Tala system, just like Raga, evolved over a period of time and it is very codified. It serves two purposes. One, to provide the accompaniment to vocal and instrumental and two, to offer a solo presentation such as in Tabla or Mridangam. Tala offers about fourteen varieties, from very slow to very fast tempo. Indian classical music is based on Raga and Tala and teaching your children these fundamentals of understanding and enjoying will help them enjoy the vast beauty of Indian classical music throughout their lives.

# Indian musical instruments

Indian musical instruments can be another great way to expose your children to the beauty of Indian music. There are so many different kinds of musical instruments from Tabla and Sitar to

Veena and Mridangam that you can choose from. Just like any other art form, the best results usually come when someone in the family is interested in the instrument. Your options may also be limited by the kinds of teachers you can find in your area, although now almost all metropolitan areas have many teachers from which to choose. The key is to decide what is the best fit for your child, start early, and follow the hard discipline.

Musical instruments can be divided into two groups: string instruments and wind instruments. String instruments have two subgroups: one that can be played with the bow and the other with fingers. Veena and Sitar are played with the fingers while violin and dilruba can be played with a bow. Shehnai and the flute belong to the wind instruments. On the other hand, Tabla and Mridangam, though can sould only one note, have a special place in Indian music in their own right. They are usually very popular with children.

## Folk dances and music

You may decide that the classical form is not suitable to your child's temperament or personality and he or she may benefit from learning a form of art that is folksier rather than classical, more popular than time-honored. There are folk dances and folk songs from almost every state in India and you may find plenty of cultural treasures hidden behind these arts as well. Some of these folk dances such as Garba and Bhangra have become very popular in America's Indian community, and learning them would give a special edge to your child when he or she becomes a teenager. The same is true for folk music. The key is to find a teacher who will interest your child and bring out the beauty in these arts. If you can find a teacher who can also give some history behind these art forms, your child may benefit immensely.

# *Food: Our Delicious Connection to Culture*

Once a friend jokingly commented that instead of grouping people according to their race, nationality, or religion, we should group them according to their eating habits. It looks like every culture has evolved around food and creates a special connection through it.

Despite what kind of culture you carry inside your heart, often it is the practical things that matter in displaying or understanding one's culture. It is true that the Indian style of cooking may not be very practical for your child's everyday life in America, but it is essential for children to know a little bit of these things so that when they become adults they can pick and choose what they would like to keep in their own households. It is the backdrop of their cultural life that will help them shape their own identity. Besides that, Indian food and fashion are becoming more in vogue in the Western world and are also more acceptable at times. So knowing about this practical side of the Indian culture will help children understand, practice, and show-off their heritage to their friends!

There are so many unique aspects to both Indian cooking and Indian dressing styles that it is not practical for us to cover it all in these pages, but what we would like to do is to bring out some points and some resources (both in terms of books and websites) where you can get more information. My goal here is to alert you to this aspect of parenting, and to help you make your own decision as to how much and what you would like to teach your children.

# Cooking and teaching about spices

Recently while visiting Kerala — the spice capital of India and maybe of the whole world –we took a guided tour of spice garden. When our tour guide pointed out the medicinal benefits of as every spice typically used in Indian cooking along with the reason it is used, our teenage daughters became especially interested in these spices. Once they could see how these spices could benefit their hair, skin, and health, they were intrigued.

Indian food has become one of the most sought after foods in the world today and maybe rightly so. In fact, according to one report, the popularity of Indian food in England has not only surpassed any other kind of food, but many so-called Indian restaurants are now opened by non-Indians to cash in on the trend. With its rich spices and seemingly endless varieties it has all the right ingredients to please everyone. Children growing up today will have tremendous options to choose from. So it may be worth their while to familiarize themselves with Indian cooking.

**Teaching your children to cook**

The criteria about who should learn to cook and why has completely changed in last few decades — from what it meant to be cooking just one generation ago. It used to have a very loaded meaning – and therefore invoked a lot of strong emotions and attitudes – who should be cooking, in the house (girls and women, of course!) what should be cooked, when cooking can be done, what clothes to wear while cooking and how to cook. Almost all of these have changed in today's world. Women still primarily do the cooking, but more and more men are taking a very active interest. A new freedom in cooking means a lot of creativity can be added to this activity, once regarded as mundane.

There is one compelling reason why cooking should be a very important skill for anyone: It directly impacts one's health. So if you somehow impress upon your kids how creative cooking can be and how enjoyable — one of the few things where you can enjoy your own creation — and how important — it directly affects your health — there is no reason why anyone should not learn cooking.

On the other hand, I have seen so many young Indian kids in their teens and even early twenties who will not even go near the kitchen as long as they can help it.

Here are some suggestions to get your children interested in cooking:

**Start early**

If you wait till your child is in her early teens, you will have to work harder to get her interested in cooking. Start as early as four or five to get her to roll dough or stir a cake mix or bake cookies.

**Cook while your children are around**

Instead of finding time to cook while children are napping or watching TV, cook your family meals together. Make it an activity that is enjoyable right from the start.

**Be creative**

Let your children see how creative the process can be. Try different shapes and sizes for your bread. Try different ingredients for your salad. When children see your experiments and enjoy the outcome, they may be tempted to try the same. Also, that will help them see cooking as an enjoyable activity and not a chore to finish before plopping down to watch a TV program.

**Use books**

There are as many books as there are cooks — or so it seems. There are cookbooks for every kind of cooking and for every age group. Find several cookbooks that are appropriate for your children's age and taste and let them choose their favorite dinner once in a while from the book. A word of caution: Indian cookbooks written in India are often not that precise and lack simple explanations because it assumes a fundamental knowledge of Indian cooking.

**Explain key terms**

Just like any other field, Indian cooking has its own buzzwords and making your children familiar with them will make it easier for them to grasp the understanding of cooking.

**Indian spices and Ayurveda**

Historically, India is known for its spices. In fact, foreigners invaded India to get the spices and the British came to India to capitalize on the spice trade. Almost every Indian recipe calls for a special mixture of spices. More than pleasing the palate, every spice has a medicinal value. Not only that, but the combination of various spices in a precise way is also to helpful to digestion. That is why the books that contained the knowledge of cooking is called Paak *shastra* meaning the "science of cooking." Cooking was considered a precise science. Find out for yourself, if you do not know already, the medicinal value of different spices that are used in Indian cooking, and talk to your children about them when you get a chance.

You may want to make sure that your children know and understand some of the properties of various spices that are used in Indian cooking. Teach them how to identify different spices and the origin and medicinal value of these spices. They will be able to use this knowledge throughout their adult lives.

The same goes with Ayurveda — the science of life and longevity – that was developed and practiced in India for centuries. It is really a life science and more of a way to prevent sickness and enjoy health for the entire life and in that sense it differs from the typical medical science we are familiar with. There are fundamental rules, herbs and spices (many of them are incorporated in everyday cooking) that assure better health for life. Teaching your children a basic understanding of this ancient science will help them enjoy good health.

14 🪷

# In Closing

## Hindsight is 20/20

Just like any other job, parenting is something you learn as you go. Even after your children have passed a certain age, your learning does not stop. You realize that there are things that you could have done differently or not done at all. Here is some of the advice that was offered by parents who now look back upon their own parenting and recognize what they could have done better. I am sharing this to help you take advantage of that hindsight.

**Keeping a positive environment — always:**

If I had known enough about the benefits of a positive environment for a child to grow in, I would have made an extra effort to surround my children with total positivism. The value of a positive environment cannot be over emphasized. It opens the world of opportunity and allows them to nurture optimism. Surround your children with as much of a positive environment as possible. Feed them on positive thoughts and save them from cynicism and negativity as much as possible.

One hint: The life and literature of Swami Vivekananda has a very positive influence on growing minds.

**Teaching meditation and yoga:**

These tools offer so many advantages, they should be taught much earlier in life. Now there are books to teach meditation to very young children (age three and up), and the results indicate that children sleep better and have fewer nightmares. Create a time and place in your everyday routine to encourage children to have "quiet" time.

**Teaching the value of failure:**

We all know that unless you try you cannot achieve anything and the bigger the goals, the higher the possibility of failure. However, to let our children try many things without fear of failure is a very essential part of parenting that often we forget. We should let children feel that no matter how many things he fails at, the fact that he is trying is, and should be, good enough.

**Instill fearlessness:** In order to discipline children we often tend to create fears in their minds without realizing the damage that is being done. Swami Vivekananda has stressed the value of fearlessness, and looking back I feel that it is one of the most important gifts we can give to children. Fear is nothing but mental weakness and fearlessness is a sign of strong mind.

**Teach them to be polite but firm:**

Being polite is valued in every culture and Indian culture is no exception, but to be polite and yet firm requires a skill that may be worth cultivating. This is, of course, part of character-building when you know what needs to be done and do it in the face of social opposition. Your children will learn from your example how to disagree with someone and yet respect their views.

# Tips from grandparents

Here are some tips that came from grandparents who are actively involved in their grandchildren's lives. Today's parents can benefit from their collective wisdom.

- Children are like sponges. They absorb everything from around them. Let them absorb your values from your actions.

- Take a goal-oriented approach to parenting. Visualize how you want to see them twenty-five years from today and act accordingly.

- Teach them to distinguish between what is Shreya (Joy) and what is Preya (fun). Shreya is everlasting while preya is temporary.

- Keep an altar, no matter how small, at home; spirituality cannot be taught without practicing.

- Have a regular routine in your household that a child can observe you do, be it lighting a lamp or offering prayers or reciting a sloka.

- Sign up your child's birthday with one of the temples in India who will not only offer a special prayer on that day but will also send some token (*Bili patra*, or *bhasma*) to your child.

- Invite guests and spiritual leaders to your home whenever you get the chance because often they can explain certain concepts much more clearly than you can. Just their presence in your home will create an environment that your children can benefit from.

- Extended families play a big role in teaching children how to resolve conflict, how to show respect, and how to communicate. If you have the opportunity, expose your children to the larger family environment whenever possible.

- If grandparents are around, make sure that your children can spend some time with them. They offer a tremendous treasure of information, stories, and wisdom. Often grandparents share the part of their lives that they have not shared with their own children.

- You cannot teach your children about *"karma yoga"* or *"bhakti yoga,"* but you can practice it. Your children will learn from your practice more than your lectures.

- Help them create their own connections with their long distance cousins and grandparents by suggesting they make phone calls or write letters themselves. Eventually they will learn to own up to these relationships.

# *Epilogue*

It is ironic that I am writing this last part of the book within weeks of our youngest one leaving for college and experiencing an empty nest for the first time. In some ways, I feel that it is giving me a good perspective on parenting as I feel that my active parenting days are over and it is a new chapter in our lives with long-distance parenting. Also, it is allowing me to look at some of the issues discussed in this book with the virtue of distance and time where I can look at them with more objectivity and examine what we could have done, what is it that we did that brought better results, and what our friends and peers did that worked as well. I have been able to see what worked so far and what I could have done better; I have a network of friends and family members who also are seeing their children off to colleges and looking at life ahead. No doubt, the roles of parents change, as children become grown-ups themselves and the quality of relationships change but the love and caring remains intact.

As any parent will testify, parenting is a life-long occupation and even when you have stopped playing active roles in the lives of your children, you are still a very important influence. In fact, you become their role model in how to strive for the best, achieve and digest the successes, how to learn from mistakes and ultimately, how to enjoy old age.

Interestingly my husband and I started thinking about these issues way before we had children of our own, only because, as a volunteer at a youth camp for Indian kids. I remember discussing so many issues that were very high on the minds and hearts of the parents at that time. Today, when I see those kids as adults in their late twenties and early thirties, married, raising their own children I cannot help feeling a sense of gratitude and faith that despite our day-to-day concerns children do turn out fine.

I only make this point to calm some of the anxieties that we carry as parents and to emphasize the benefit of long term perspective.

May you the reader benefit from the hindsight that is provided in this book and enjoy the never-ending fruits of being a parent. It is interesting how our children provide us with a new insight into our lives and allow us to come full circle in terms of understanding our own parents and grandparents.

Happy parenting!

— Meenal Pandya

# Appendix

## Helpful books and websites

*A World of Babies* by Judy DeLoache and Alma Goetlieb

*Building Moral Intelligence: The Seven Essential Virtues that Teach Kids To Do the Right Thing* by Michele Borba

*How to Talk So Kids Will Listen and Listen So Kids Will Talk* by Adele Faber and Elaine Mazlish

*Counseling the Culturally Different: Theory and Practice* by Derald Wing Sue and Davis Sue

*Kids Online* by Donna Rice Hughes

*Raising the Rainbow Generation: Teaching your Children in a Multicultural Society.* By Dr. Darlene Hopson

*Too Much of a Good Thing: Raising Children of Character in an Indulgent Age* by Daniel J Kindlon

*Positive Discipline for Teenagers* by Jane Nelson and Lynn Lott.

*The 7 Secrets of Successful Parents* by Randy Rolfe

*Using Your Values to Raise Your Child To Be an Adult You Admire* by Harriet Heath. published by Parenting Press, Inc. Seattle Washington.

*Passage from India: Post 1965 Indian Immigrants and Their Children, Conflicts, Concerns and Solutions* by Priya Agarwal.

*Raising Good Children* by Dr. Thomas Likona.

*Raising a Secure Child: Creating an Emotional Connection between You and Your Child* by Zeynep Biringen.

*Moonbeam: A book of meditations for children Simple Visualizations for Parents to Help Children to Awaken Creativity, Sleep Peacefully, Develop Concentration, and Quiet Fears.* By Maureen Garth.

*Raising Your Child to be a Champion in Athletics, Arts, and Academics* by Wayne Bryan and Woody Woodburn.

*Indian Classical Dance: Tradition in Transition* by Leela Venkataraman and Avinash Pasricha.

# Internet Resources

http://www.Indiaparenting.com/

Although this website is designed by women in New Delhi India, it has some information that is useful to all Indian parents irrespective of where they live.

http://www.4to40.com/contents.htm

A nice site for a lot of information on Indian mythological and historical stories.

http://www.parenting.com/parenting/

http://www.parenting.org/

http://www.parenthood.com/links.html

http://www.positiveparenting.com/

http://www.activeparenting.com/

http://parentingtoolbox.com/

http://www.hinduismtoday.com/

http://www.kahani.com/

http://www.hinduschools.org/

http://www.indianmoms.com/about.htm

http://www.all-india-tour-travel.com/
dances/bharatanatyam.htm

http://www.angelfire.com/al/saree/

This is a good website, if you are interested in teaching yourself or your daughter about Sari, how to wear it, what are the different styles etc.

http://www.himalayanacademy.com/

# Indian Calendar

Indian Calendar is based on lunar cycle. Each month consists of two fortnights and begins with new moon. At the end of full moon, the second fortnight begins and the month ends on the no moon day.

Twelve months, and their important festivals are:

1. Karttika Diwali/Vikram Samvat New Year

2. Margashirsha

3. Pausha

4. Magha Pongal/Vasant Panchmi

5. Phaluguna Holi/Maha Shivratri

6. Chaitra Ramnavmi

7. Vaishakha

8. Jyestha

9. Ashadha

10. Shravana Raksha Bandhan/Janmashtami

11. Badra

12. Ashvina Navratri/Durga Pooja/Diwali

# Looking at time from the Indian perspective

Indian calendar looks at time in a cyclical way and defines cosmic cycles — Kalpas and Yugas — for the calculation of age of the universe. According to this cosmic cycle is one of the infinitely recurring periods of the universe, comprising its creation, preservation and dissolution.

In each Kalpa, there are four Yugas — Satya, Treta, Dwapar, and Kali.

These four Yugas make one Mahayuga (4,320,000 years).

71 Mahayugas make one Manvantara.

14 Manvantaras make one day of creator Brahma (Kalpa)

2 Kalpas make one Ahortra

360 Ahoratra make one year of Brahma.

According to Puranas current period is in the Kali Yuga of $28^{th}$ Mahayuga of $51^{st}$ Brahma year.

# Some facts about India

| | |
|---|---|
| **Area:** | 3.3 million square kilometers |
| **Coastline:** | 7600 km |
| **Languages:** | 17 major languages, 844 dialects |
| **Major religions:** | Hinduism, Buddhism, Sikhism, Jainism, Islam, and Christianity |
| **National Emblem:** | Replica of the Lion Capital of Sarnath |
| **National Flag:** | Horizontal tricolor in equal proportion of deep saffron on the top, white in the middle and dark green at the bottom. In the center of the white band is a wheel in a navy blue color. |
| **National Animal:** | Panthera tigris |
| **National Bird:** | Peacock |
| **National Flower:** | Lotus |
| **National Tree:** | Banyan tree |
| **National Fruit:** | Mango |
| **National Currency:** | Rupees |
| **Political Structure:** | Sovereign, Socialist, Secular, Democratic Republic |
| **The Indian Union:** | 26 states and six centrally-administered Union Territories |

**Form of Government:** Parliamentary, based on universal adult franchise

**Legislature:** Parliament consists of President and the two Houses, known as Rajya Sabha (Council of States) and Lok Sabha (House of the People) Executive consists of President, Vice President and council of Ministers led by the Prime Minister

**Judiciary:** Independent of executive

# Glossary

**Aarti**   Offering of lighted lamps usually in a plate to a deity.

**Arangetram**   Culmination of Bharatnatyam dance training where the student performs on the stage in front of the teacher and family members.

**Ashram**   A retreat for spiritual studies.

**Avyakta**   Unmanifested .

**Bhajan**   Devotional singing.

**Bhakti yoga**   Yoga of devotion.

**Bhangra**   Folk dance from Punjab, a northern state in India.

**Bhasma**   Ashes or powder from the holy fire.

**Bili patra**   Triple leaves purported to be the favorite of Lord Shiva.

**Bindi (tilak)**   Vermillion dot on the center of one's forehead.

**Brahmacharyaashram**   The first 25 years of one's life where the goal is to excel in studies and maintain celibacy.

**Carnataki**   Indian classical music from south.

**Dharma**   Social code of conduct.

**Dilruba**   Bowed string musical instrument.

**Diwali**   Hindu festival of lights.

**Dusera**  Hindu festival that signifies Sri Rama's victory.

**Ganesha**  Hindu God who is believed to be the remover of obstacles.

**Garba**  Folk dance from Gujarat.

**Gita**  Hindu Spiritual book, also known as Bhagvad Gita.

**Gujarati**  A state language of Gujarat.

**Haldi**  Turmeric powder .

**Havan Pooja**  Offering to a deity in front of a Holy fire.

**Hindustani**  North Indian classical music.

**Karma yoga**  Yoga of Action.

**Kerala**  South-western coastal state in India.

**Kumkum**  Vermillion powder.

**Lord Shiva**  One of the Gods of trinity that is known as the god of destruction.

**Lord Vishnu**  One of the gods of trinity that is known as the god of preservation.

**Mahabharata**  Hindu epic.

**Mala**  Rosary .

**Maryada**  Social code of distinction between appropriate and inappropriate.

**Mausi**  Mother's sister.

**Mridang**  A percussion instrument from southern India.

**Panchtantra**  Collection of stories where important ethical and moral lessons are taught through animal stories .

**Pooja**  Deity worship.

**Prakriti**  One's innate nature.

**Raga**  Melodic composition.

**Ramayana**  Hindu epic.

**Sanskrit**  India's ancient language.

**Sanskruti**  Culture.

**Saraswati**  Goddess of knowledge.

**Satyanarayan pooja**  Worship of Lord Satyanarayan.

**Shehnai**  Wind musical instrument.

**Sitar**  String musical instrument.

**Slokas**  Religious hymns.

**Tabla**  Percussion Instrument similar to drums.

**Tala**  Musical composition based on rhythm.

**Vasudhaiva Kutumbakam**  Hindu saying that means "The entire earth is one family".

**Vedas**  Ancient books of wisdom .

**Veena**   String musical instrument.

**Vidya**   Knowledge.

**Vijaya dasmi**   A Hindu festival, also known as Dusera.

**Vikruti**   Perversion.

**Vyakti**   An Individual.

# Bibliography

Pasricha Avinash and Venkataraman, Leela. *Indian Classical Dance: Tradition in Transition.* Lustre Press Roli Books

Borba, Michele. *Building Moral Intelligence: The Seven Essential Virtues that Teach kids To Do the Right Thing.* Jossey-Bass.

Agarwal, Priya. *Passage from India: Post 1965 Indian Immigrants and Their Children, Conflicts, Concerns and Solutions.* Yuvati Publications.

Faber, Adele and Mazlish, Elaine. *How to Talk So Kids Will Listen and Listen So Kids Will Talk.* HarperResource.

Bryan, Wayne and Woodburn, Woody. *Raising Your Child to be a Champion in Athletics, Arts, and Academics* Citadel Press

Rolfe, Randy *The 7 Secrets of Successful Parents.* Contemporary Books.

Joshi, Baburao. *Understanding Indian Music.* Asia Publishing House.

Harding, Edith and Riley, Philip *The Bilingual Family: A Handbook for Parents.* University Press.

You cannot teach a child anymore than you can grow a plant. The plant develops its own nature. The child also teaches itself. But you can help it to go forward in its own way. What you can do is not of positive nature but negative. You can take away the obstacles, and knowledge comes out of its own nature. Loosen the soil a little so that it may come out easily. Put a hedge around it; see that it is not killed by anything. You can supply the growing seed with material for the marketing up of its body, bringing to it the earth, the water, the air that it wants. And there your work stops. It will take all that it wants by its own nature.

## swami vivekananda

# About the Author

Meenal Pandya has been writing about India and its culture for almost two decades observing the lifestyle and issues of Indians living outside of India. She is also highly involved with cultural issues within the Indian immigrant community through seminars and community organizations. Meenal has earned MBA in Finance and works as a consultant in the Boston area. She has been living in the U.S. for last thirty years and has raised two daughters. Meenal has written four books and hundreds of articles touching on the issues of the cultural life of Indians.

Other books by Meenal Pandya

*Pick a Pretty Indian Name for Your Baby*

*Here Comes Diwali: The Festival of Light*

*Here Comes Holi: The Festival of Colors*

*Vivah: Design a Perfect Hindu Wedding*